Tales of the Popes

From Eden to El Dorado

An Infamous History

LARRY BUTTROSE

NEW
HOLLAND

for my mother, my sister Mary-Anne
and my niece Hayley,
and for Belle

CONTENTS

INTRODUCTION

This book is a popular history for the general reader. It is a book for all those who may have wondered what the Borgias did to acquire such infamy, who the Medici and the antipopes were, and who was responsible for the cruelty of the Inquisition. All these questions are linked to the papacy of the Roman Catholic Church, and indeed there were Borgia popes and Medici popes. In dealing with such intriguing and often extreme figures, I have worked to bring them back to life as characters in a book which deals with popes as men, rather than simply religious figureheads. As such, this is a work which considers the papacy as a human institution, very human, with all the flaws and failings, and the intelligence and resourcefulness, of humans.

Tales of the Popes covers the papacy up to the year 1600, ending with the burning at the stake of the free thinker and philosopher Giordano Bruno, at the order of a pope. It concludes at that year, not only because by then many of the most remarkable papal episodes have taken place, but because after the sixteenth century the Church begins its decline in real power against the rational assertion of the Enlightenment, the wealth of banks and armies of nations, the momentous changes in science and technology, and the make-up of human societies, political structures and cultures. Until the sixteenth century, popes stood front and centre in European affairs. They commanded armies, conducted Inquisitions and burned alive those who disagreed with their views. From the seventeenth century onwards though, the papacy began to assume more the role of spiritual guide and ethical advisor, starting its gradual transformation towards a kind of transnational agony aunt, with plenty of moral huff and puff but little if any real temporal thwack. Although any organisation with a billion members will of necessity wield great influence, and the papacy certainly retains that, compare its importance in everyday life with, say, Google—not to mention the internet itself—and one gets an idea of how much has changed. The carbon credit of today is the papal indulgence of centuries past.

✠ ✠ ✠

There was no Pope in Eden, and none was present at the pillage of the Americas, the fabled 'El Dorado', yet neither story would have the same import for us now without the papacy. The tale of Eden, the earthly paradise from which, according to Christian belief, disgraced humanity fell, comes down to us bearing the imprimatur of two millennia of pontiffs.

It is also worth noting that according to The Book of Genesis, God made Adam in his own image. As such, Adam became the first representation of God on Earth. Later, that representation would be provided by 'God's Vicar on Earth, the Pope'. These two usages of 'representation' may at first appear disingenuous, but I would suggest that Adam did have much in common with a pope, being the man with whom God was most directly connected (in Adam's case, according to the Bible, until God fashioned Eve from his rib, he was the only person on Earth). Thus the interweaving of human destiny with the intention of the divinity was articulated through Adam, just as later it would be for all of Christendom by the pope.

That same pope was the Vicar of the God whom the Spanish Conquistadors, the conquerors of the New World, invoked as they plundered the gold of the Aztecs and Incas, and dreamed of yet more for the taking in El Dorado. There was a missionary zeal to their quest, the reaping of souls seemingly as important to some as the gold itself: but gold has always exercised a unique hold upon the imaginations of people, whether pioneers, privateers or pontiffs.

The Conquistadors brought back heady tales of remote cities covered with gold, and peoples of colossal wealth, such as the Muisca of Colombia, who ritually gilded the heir to the throne, the 'El Dorado', meaning literally the 'gilded one'. The popular meaning of El Dorado as a legendary place of untold wealth is an extension of this original meaning. In the account from 1589 of Spanish adventurer Jaun de Castellanos, the Muisca king was presented 'naked ... coated totally with resin, and over that a quantity of gold dust ... '[1] The title given to the king would one day represent to the Spanish all the riches for the taking in the New World. 'Consequently El Dorado gradually became a general term referring to various places of possible treasure, a mirage luring many on expeditions of conquest.'[2]

The quantity and the value of plunder taken from the Americas through bloodshed and enslavement of the native populations was without precedent. 'According to official reports of the Spanish colonial administration, about a century after the beginning of the conquest of America, 181 tons of gold and 16,000 tons of silver had been brought to Spain from the American colonies. The sudden influx of artificial wealth, causing unprecedented inflation in Europe, was a vital factor in the creation and maintenance of the Spanish empire, one of the most powerful ever known in world history.'[3]

By the time the Conquistadors had finished, entire peoples had been left shattered, cultures lost and native populations worked to death mining their own lands beneath the lash of their captors. And as we shall see, no matter how the popes may have felt about the tragedy they knew was unfolding, it had all begun with the stroke of a papal pen. Such was the power over human fate wielded by the pope.

✧ ✧ ✧

Together the popes comprise the chain of command of the oldest corporate entity on earth. The Popes—all 262 of them, up to and including the current Pope, Benedict XVI—lay claim to a 2000 year lineage back to Saint Peter, the 'rock' upon which Jesus Christ is said to have founded his church. In those two intervening millennia, the Church that Peter founded has spread and prospered, in terms of its religious and moral message, its wealth, and its abiding influence. Popes may no longer lead armies on horseback, but presidents, kings and prime ministers still make their way to the Vatican for an audience with the pontiff.

The Church, which the popes have ruled, is in many respects as Roman as it is catholic (universal), inheriting the Roman Empire's executive authority and bureaucracy, as well as its language, and a penchant for secrecy and real estate. To some observers, the Pope waving in white from his balcony in Saint Peter's Square remains in essence the ruler of an Empire which never quite fell, still with fabulous riches from across the four corners of the world, even if nowadays the means of control is a body of texts, rather than the sword. But then, in the beginning was The Word.

While the Pope possesses the absolute executive authority of a Roman emperor, the position is elected (sometimes subject to outside lobbying, deal-making, bribery and corruption) like a consul of the old Roman Republic. Considering the degree to which nepotism was rife for many centuries, it is nonetheless to the Church's credit that the position of pope remained elected,

and never became merely dynastic.

The early popes often had short lives, far removed from the pomp and celebrity of modern pontiffs. Early Christians lived in the shadow of torture and death at the hands of their Roman masters, and to be a pope in the first three hundred years of the church was a risky business: the first three popes were martyred. During the Middle Ages popes were renowned as pious saints and terrible sinners. Popes did lead armies into battle, had rivals tortured and murdered, indulged in financial corruption, excess and debauchery, fathered offspring and kept concubines. There were popes and antipopes, competing popes in Rome and Avignon dividing their church. Yet they also acted as stewards over scholarship and literature, and in their own manner contributed to the gradual advancement of humankind towards a more orderly and just society.

In their time popes have been witness to, and more often than not been entwined in, the Byzantine and Holy Roman Empires, mediaeval Europe through the so-called Dark Ages, the horrors of the Inquisition and the Reformation and Counter-Reformation, the artistic zenith of the Renaissance and the conquest and plundering of the New World, the Enlightenment debates of philosophy, science and cosmology, the French Revolution and the Industrial Revolution, the rise of European fascism and fall of the Soviet Union, and the arrival of the digital era. As key players in the human drama of 2000 years—almost half of recorded history—popes have touched almost every human society in some way or another. When the Pope speaks, his one billion followers, as well as many millions of others, listen. The intense global media coverage of the death of Pope Jean-Paul II in 2005 demonstrated the power and public fascination the papacy still commands among Catholics, Protestants and non-Christians alike. The media posse which follows Pope Benedict everywhere he goes attests that the public fascination with the papacy continues into the Church's third millennium.

Popes are often outspoken on controversial matters such as the relationship between medical science and ethics, ongoing debates on birth control, abortion and euthanasia, as well as HIV/AIDS, capital punishment, war and nuclear weaponry, terrorism, and the legitimacy of religion at all in a secular world. These are concerns of people everywhere, whether one agrees with a papal opinion or not. As such, popes articulate a range of issues confronting the world as it is, sometimes with greater clarity than other leaders whose political or economic allegiance may be more manifest. Popes might once have endorsed red hot irons and burning at the stake for those who failed to share their opinions, but their two thousand years of survival is also testament to their nous, subtlety and sophistication. With continuing global interest, and their great numbers of followers, it would appear they will abide for some time to come.

This book will investigate the strongest and most intriguing stories of the papacy, through the most colourful eras of its history. It is by no means intended as a definitive or even thorough account: that requires an encyclopaedia. Instead, this is a collection of stories based upon the lives of certain of the popes, those who have come down the generations to be regarded as some of the most courageous or visionary, vexed by historical events, or self-servingly treacherous and corrupt: the good, the bad and the ugly. As such, it is a book about humanity as it is, or as it is specifically in this case, men as they are, the popes being men to a man.

I hope this book serves to enlighten the reader about this unique human institution, as well as to inform, and entertain.

Larry Buttrose

I. IN THE BEGINNING

The Papacy is no other than the ghost of the deceased Roman empire, sitting crowned upon the grave thereof.

—THOMAS HOBBES

Such is the authority attached to the office of Pope that there is no aspect of the Roman Catholic Church, and Christianity in general, which does not reflect in some way the influence of the living Pope, and the lineage of the hundreds which preceded him. The Pope or pontiff is the direct descendent of the office of the *pontifex maximus*, the religious leader of the Romans. As the position of pontifex maximus merged with that of the Emperor in the time of Julius Caesar, the Pope is also inheritor of that dual role, of the civil and religious leadership of ancient Rome. Indeed, so the theory goes, blink and the Pope in white waving from his balcony in the Vatican is very much like Caesar in his toga, waving to the Roman populace. Historians have a term for this, *caesaropapism*.

The lineage itself is of unique human historical importance, perhaps the oldest absolute monarchy in the world, and that monarch has ruled over vast populations and territories. There is no equivalent in Judaism, Islam, Hinduism or the Eastern Orthodox Church to a pope, no figure of such centrality and absolute authority.

If the pope is indeed the rebadged Emperor of Rome, his domain became an empire of sorts far greater than Augustus or Claudius could ever have imagined. In a sense, the Roman Empire did not suffer its fall, but evolved from military imperialism into an evangelistic entity. The very title pontifex maximus or 'supreme priest', which used to belong to the emperor, became that of the popes, and remains so, with Benedict XVI the current pontifex maximus.

Yet, of course, this is only one small aspect of the very beginning of the story, the first word, as it were, for while the pope may indeed be seen by some as the emperor in new clothes, the empire over which he presides is very different—a philosophical, ethical and legal system with a two thousand year history.

How did the global religion of Roman Catholicism develop from an anthology of colourful stories of tribal peoples in ancient western Asia? The answer is in part Greek philosophy and part Roman law, but there is, needless to say, far more to add to that mix, including Judaism, and various forms of mysticism. In many regards the key to any understanding of Roman Catholicism is a consideration of how authority operates within it, in terms of its liturgy and dogma, and its executive powers. Central to an understanding of those is the role of the pope. In other words, in Catholicism all roads lead to Rome, and more particularly, to the Vatican.

✠　✠　✠

Beyond the Gospel accounts of the New Testament of the Bible, letters of Saint Paul and some Roman references, little is known about the Jewish spiritual leader called Jeshua Ben Joseph, or Jesus Christ, who was executed on a charge of sedition by the Romans in Jerusalem in the fourth decade of the Common Era. The Gospels record that he was born in Palestine, into the family of a carpenter, and was taken for a time to Egypt by his parents, fleeing Herod's Massacre of the Innocents.

Jesus later lived in Nazareth, visited Jerusalem, and as a young man of some learning began to assemble a group of disciples around him. He preached a creed of compassion and non-violence to his growing flock of followers, and the Gospels provide accounts of him delivering speeches to people in their thousands, and of working miracles such as raising people from the dead and curing diseases and afflictions. He questioned aspects of the Jewish faith, and claimed to be the son of God, though how literal this claim was intended to be is questionable. Like many of the mysteries surrounding Jesus and the foundation of the Christian faith, his words have been hostage to many generations of writing and re-writing, translation and editing, deletion, censorship, accidental loss and wilful destruction.

He travelled through Palestine preaching a message of compassion and forgiveness to ever-larger crowds, his popularity rapidly increasing. It appears he particularly found appeal as he exalted the poor, and said that it would be easier for the rich 'to pass through the eye of a needle' than to enter the Kingdom of Heaven. He also consorted with outcasts, thieves and prostitutes, and believed women should be accorded respect, a view as alien in his day as it remains to many elements of today's world. It was however the claim that he was 'King of the Jews' which led to his downfall and death.

After Jesus and his disciples arrived in Jerusalem to a massed welcome and great public excitement, and drove the bankers from the Temple, he was soon betrayed by Judas, one of his inner circle. Brought before a Jewish court on a charge of blasphemy, he was hauled before the Roman procurator Pontius Pilate, where the charge became sedition, for the claim that he was King of the Jews. Whether Jesus had meant this only in a spiritual or allegorical way, or whether he had really been trying to organise some kind of insurrection against Roman rule, remains as debatable today as it might have been to the Romans. Their method of dealing with him was brutal, however, and Jesus was sentenced to immediate death by crucifixion. Christians believe that Jesus triumphed over death by coming back to life three days later, and allowing himself to be seen by some of his followers, before ascending into the heavens, where he rejoined God, his father.

The followers of Jesus began to spread the doctrine of compassion of their departed leader. Peter (called Simon) was named in the Gospels as the 'first' among the Apostles, and so it is not surprising that he became recognised as the head of the nascent religious body. According to the Gospel of Matthew, Jesus said: 'You are Peter, and on this rock (*petros*, Greek for rock) I will build my church.' The Gospel of John indicates the same leadership role for Peter, with Jesus imploring him to 'feed my lambs', and to 'tend my sheep', the ovine metaphor for his flock of followers.

Peter travelled north from Jerusalem on a journey through the desert which would take him to Antioch in Syria, Greece, and finally Rome. Along the way he gathered followers to this new faith, as did another apostle who reached Rome, Paul. The Romans found the cult something of an annoyance, pitting as it did its single god against the might of the Roman pantheon, and its doctrine of compassion against the visceral realpolitik of Roman imperial rule. Peter and Paul both met grisly fates on the same day in Rome, 29 June 67 CE, Peter crucified upside down and Paul beheaded, both upon the orders of Emperor Nero.[1]

Like Jesus and Peter, many of the early Christians and their pontiffs died agonising deaths by crucifixion.[2] In addition to crucifixion, the Romans often used wild animals against their foes, some early popes thrown to beasts in the arena. Others were even turned into blazing human torches to light the public games.

'Nero had self-acknowledged Christians arrested. Then, on their information, large numbers of others were condemned—not so much for incendiarism as for their anti-social tendencies. Their deaths were made farcical. Dressed in wild animals' skins, they were torn to pieces by dogs, or crucified, or made into torches to be ignited after dark as substitutes for daylight. Nero provided his Gardens for the spectacle, and exhibited displays in the Circus, at which he mingled with the crowd—or stood in a chariot, dressed as a charioteer. Despite their guilt as Christians, and the ruthless punishment it deserved, the victims were pitied. For it was felt that they were being sacrificed to one man's brutality rather than the national interest.'[3]

Not all Romans treated early Christians with the brutality we have often seen in Hollywood films. However, some of this impression derived from the excesses of deranged rulers such as Nero. A defining aspect of Roman life was Roman law,[4] and an illustration of how the Roman legal system, when properly adhered to, treated early Christians, is contained in a letter from Emperor Trajan to the historian Pliny the younger, then a provincial governor, circa 100 CE.

You have followed the correct procedure, dear Secundus, in investigating the cases of those who were accused in your court of being

Christians. It is not possible to lay down a rule that can be universally applicable, in a set of words. They are not to be hunted out; and who are accused and convicted should be punished, with the proviso that if a man says that he is not a Christian and makes it obvious by his actual conduct, namely by worshipping our gods, when, however suspect he may have been with regard to the past, he should gain pardon from his repentance. No anonymous lists that are submitted should carry weight in any charges. That would be the worst of precedents and out of keeping with the spirit of our age.[5]

Much of the early era of the Church was spent in doctrinal argument, a pastime which would long bedevil it. Such matters as the Trinity, inscribed by early Christians such as Saint Augustine[6] (Augustine of Hippo 354–430, the Algerian-born son of a Roman soldier), would become a cornerstone of the faith.[7] Other issues included the Eucharist, or Holy Communion[8], and the Virgin Birth, the belief Mary gave birth to Jesus while she was still a virgin.[9] Given the subject matter of such beliefs, it is little wonder that these and other aspects of the dogma and ritual of the early Church proved thorny. Later thinkers such as the Italian Saint Thomas Aquinas (1225–1274) would seek to expand the philosophical breadth of Church doctrine, seeking a reconciliation with the philosophy of Aristotle, and attempting to prove the existence of God through reason.[10]

During the early period of the Church the liturgy was recited, sung, even whispered at gatherings in catacombs and other secret locations. For the first four hundred years of the church, it was recited in Greek, from Illyria to Gaul and North Africa. When the Bible was translated from Greek to Latin in the mid fourth century of the Common Era—the *Itala*, which later appeared as the *Vulgate*—what may have been encouragement to good deeds in

Greek took on the timbre and cadence of Roman law, with all its proscriptive overtones in the Latin language.

Despite this, up until recent decades, the Greek origins of the Bible were still recognised in services at the Vatican. 'At Solemn Papal Masses today in St Peter's the Epistle and Gospel are read first in Latin and then in Greek'.[11] This Greek influence remains to the present day in Catholic liturgy, with the chanted prayer 'Kyrie Eleison, Christe Eleison' or 'Lord Have Mercy, Christ Have Mercy'.

After Peter, the Tuscan cleric Linus was the second pope, from 67–76 CE, followed by Anacletus (also called Cletus), from 76–88 CE. Some accounts of Anacletus say that he served twice as pope, his papacy interrupted by banishment from Rome. He constructed the tomb of Saint Peter at the Vatican, across the Tiber from city of Rome, and both he and Linus were buried nearby following their martyrdom. Both were canonised. Linus and Anacletus were Bishops of Rome, but they were not then considered to have more authority than any other bishop.

Peter has been named as the first Bishop of Rome, perhaps with more political expediency than historical truth: the lives of the apostles generated a great deal of legend. He cannot really have been a pope, because at this time the office of pontifex maximus was occupied by a pagan Roman. Nevertheless, the Bishops of Rome were eager to establish their legitimacy as first among equals very early in the Church's history.

Clement (pope 88–97 CE), now known as the fourth pope, propagated the theory that Jesus, and therefore God, had personally chosen Peter to be Bishop of Rome. This theory was later called the Petrine Primacy. Thus all of Peter's successors in that office, including Clement himself, enjoyed similar divine approval, an advantage other bishops could not claim.

Popes continued to live risky lives for the next two centuries, and it wasn't until Miltiades gained the backing of the newly converted Roman Emperor Constantine in the year 312 that the institution of the papacy as we know it now, came into being. The teachings of Christ as recounted in the Gospels give his followers the liturgical basis for their faith, but the conversion of Constantine some three centuries later was a watershed, a critical event which guaranteed the survival of the church Jesus founded with his Apostles.

Constantine was born Flavius Valerius Constantinus in 280 CE at Naissus, now Nis, in modern Serbia. His father served as Deputy Emperor Constantius I Chlorus, and the young Constantine grew up in the Eastern empire, brought up in the court of Emperor Diocletian at Nicomedia (now the Turkish city of Izmit, about 100 kilometres across the Bosporus from Istanbul). He served in the military as a young man.

The abdications of Diocletian and his co-emperor Maximian in 305 triggered a lengthy power struggle in the ruling echelon of the Roman Empire, and with his son at his side Constantius led an army on a campaign into Britain. Constantius was killed in battle in northern England, at Eboracum (now York), in 306, and Constantine was immediately acclaimed as emperor by his troops. Six years later, in 312, Constantine fought a crucial battle, at the Milvian Bridge near Rome, and it was at this time that he made his conversion from the Roman to the Christian religion. A number of accounts tell how this occurred. One is that he had a dream in which the shields of his troops were painted with the Christian symbol; another is he had a vision of the Christian symbol across the sky, accompanied by the motif 'In this sign conquer'. With the Edict of Milan (313)[12] guaranteeing religious freedom across the Roman world, Christianity had gone from a cult among desert-dwellers at the far end of the empire to the religion of the Roman Emperor, practised throughout the empire.

Perhaps at the Battle of Milvian Bridge, Constantine did not so much see the writing in the sky, as on the wall. Despite three centuries of often vicious suppression, the Christian cult still flourished across the Roman Empire and was, if anything, gaining strength. Despite a final attempt by Diocletian to subdue it in the time of the young Constantine, the cult retained its vigour and popular appeal, and there had been rumours of leading Romans taking secret conversions.

It is possible that Constantine saw in Christianity a way to unite a disparate empire stretching from the snows of Britain to the desert wastes of Asia Minor. After all, if Christianity had such appeal to widely scattered and greatly varying peoples that it could withstand the skills of Roman torturers, perhaps it could flourish across the empire and bind it together.

Constantine had a precedent for this in the ancient warrior king who did something very similar, Alexander the Great (356–323 BCE). The young Macedonian had conquered half the known world, only to die while still a young man in the world's oldest city, Babylon. The young prince Alexander was tutored by Aristotle, whose teaching helped mould his character, and was inspired to seek greatness by the verses of Homer. After the assassination of his father, Phillip II, he set out on his father's long-planned war with rival power Persia in 333 BCE. In a series of military triumphs, he defeated the Persian king Darius, conquering Persia, Syria and Egypt, and continuing to campaign westwards he reached India, which he believed to be the limit of the world.

He reinforced his rule throughout his many realms by the introduction of a single currency, his image on every coin, and also through a merging of religions in his realm into something approaching a single creed. This was exemplified by his willingness to merge the Greek god Zeus with the god Amon of his Egyptian subjects.

'Hearing that his reputed ancestors Perseus and Heracles had visited the famous oracle of the chief Egyptian god Amon at the western oasis of Siwah, Alexander sought glory for himself by making the dangerous pilgrimage deep into the desert. At the oasis the prophet of the god received Alexander and greeted him, according to one account, as 'Son of Amon', for as king of Egypt he was officially divine. The Macedonians and Greeks had long identified Amon with Zeus, under the name Zeus Amon, and stories began to circulate among them that Alexander had been hailed as Son of Zeus. Apparently Alexander's pilgrimage to the oracular seat had a profound impression on him. Thenceforth he turned increasingly towards his divine sonship of Zeus Amon as a means of binding all his subjects to his rule … A figure of his exalted status, a hero with a mortal mother and divine father, was thought to have the power to see into heaven, and Alexander was often depicted in art or on coins staring upward into the divine realm.'[13]

In styling himself as son of the god Zeus, but also as the son of a mortal queen, Alexander had wrought a trinity of a kind from his own life, and this trinity may have served as an inspiration for the Christian one to come centuries later. At the same time it has also been opined that his death, at age 33, may have provided a model for the Church for the age of Jesus at the time of his death.[14] Certainly, with the passing of six centuries the legend of Alexander had reached mythic proportions, so that by the time of Constantine, Alexander the Great's almost superhuman deeds could not fail but to inspire, and to be examined minutely, and perhaps imitated.

Similarly then it would not be such a leap for the man who would unite the Western and Eastern Roman Empires, and all their far-flung peoples with their many faiths, under the banner of a religion which simply would not go away no matter what the Romans brought against it. Its appeal had stood the test of time: it had been tested with fire and steel. Why not then, Constantine might well have thought, unite all the empire beneath its cross?

He did just that, defeating Emperor Licinius in 324 and becoming sole emperor of the Eastern and Western empires. Next Constantine called the Council of Nicaea in 325 to help codify the Christian creed, and chose Byzantium as the capital of the unified Roman Empire, renaming it Constantinople in 330.

Constantine believed his duty as a Christian also lay in the proper administration of the earthly realm of Rome, and greatly improved the running of the re-integrated Empire. By the time of his death, so entrenched had Christianity become in the beliefs and daily life of the rulers and peoples of Rome, that an attempt by the later Emperor Julian to remove it failed. The Roman Empire and Christianity were now woven into one, and the stage set for the time of the popes.

2. HEAVENLY FRAUD, THE CORPSE IN THE DOCK, AND POPE JOAN

The Holy Roman Empire was neither Holy,
Roman nor an Empire.

—VOLTAIRE

Called the greatest forgery of all time, the 'Donation of Constantine' laid the foundations for papal temporal authority for more than a thousand years.[1] The notorious eighth century fake supposedly showed that Emperor Constantine 'ceded all the Western World to the Bishop of Rome and his descendants in perpetuity ... Armed with this document, successive popes persuaded successive emperors to honour the wish of their great predecessor and cede part, at least, of their Italian possessions to St Peter.'[2]

It was through its claim to these same Italian possessions, the Papal States, a belt of territories running down the middle of the 'boot' of Italy, and the 'Western regions'—the entire western empire—that the early Church was able to establish itself as an economic and imperial power. It only lost the last of them in 1870 with the unification of Italy—then regained sovereignty over the tiny territory of the State of Vatican City in 1929, with the pious beneficence of the fascist dictator Mussolini.[3]

If the 'Donation of Constantine' had not been forged it would have been necessary to forge it. The Roman Empire may have fallen, its military and territorial dominance consigned to history, and mighty and terrifying figures such as Julius Caesar, Augustus, Tiberius and Nero all gone, but in their place in Rome one man stood at the apex of a potent hierarchy, a rich historical mix of families and obligations, of tribal custom and law. In him was vested a unique combination of absolute spiritual authority, temporal might, colossal wealth and influence: the pope. And behind the pope stood the 'Donation of Constantine'.

The document, purported to have been written some five centuries before by Emperor Constantine himself, was the doing of a mid-eighth century cleric and papal official named Christophorous. To understand the circumstances of his forgery, it is necessary to go back some decades before it was uttered, to a dispute which wracked the empire, and the church.

After the converted Constantine moved the capital of the Roman empire to Constantinople, or Byzantium, in 328 CE, the focus of the Christian world shifted by degrees to the east. With its military power weakening in the west, Rome was sacked in 410 by Goths under the command of King Alaric. A few decades later it was the rampant Huns of Atilla who menaced the Eternal City, another sacking only prevented by the personal intercession of Pope Leo I, who met with Atilla and effectively bought off the attackers. While the eastern and western arms of the empire carried on arguments about fine points of dogma, Rome was exposed to more assaults and sackings at the hands of Visigoths and Vandals.

Through the fifth and sixth centuries the Italian peninsula was routinely held hostage to plunderers, and imperial Byzantium did little to stop it. Anger in the populace simmered, but finally boiled over—though not at yet another sacking, but a war over idols.

Early Christians had been opposed to the worship of idols, and gleefully smashed those of pagan Rome after its downfall. Over time, however, Christians had become attached to their own idols and icons. This came to a head in 726 when the emperor in Byzantium, Leo III—perhaps influenced by the rising Islamic world to his right—demanded that icons be smashed across the empire. When Christians refused to comply, Pope Gregory II stated why in letters to the emperor. 'It was nonsense to say that Christians had restored the idolatry of antiquity. They did not worship images but honoured them as memorials …'[4]

The future of the empire now turned on an argument about whether Christians were worshipping idols or merely honouring them. Determined to press his point, Emperor Leo went too far, and fighting erupted.

'A fierce and bloody war was fought around Ravenna. The Byzantines retreated northward and the scenes of carnage were repeated, so frightful and bloody that for six years thereafter the inhabitants of the Po valley abstained from eating the fish of the river for fear of involuntary cannibalism.'[5]

Mutual ex-communication followed mass slaughter, and when the dust finally settled, the eastern and western parts of the empire were effectively separate entities. But who would now rule the temporal affairs of Italy? Who had that right, and by what permission? Enter then the cleric Christophorous, with his 'Donation of Constantine'.

The 'Donation of Constantine' is thought to have been forged around 754, when Pope Stephen II appealed to the Frankish

king Pepin the Short for help against the threat to Rome from the
Lombards to the north. Pepin dutifully defeated the Lombards,
seizing land they had captured from Rome, and other territories
in the central Italian peninsula, and his bequeathing of these
territories to the pope became known as the 'Donation of Pepin'.
But to legitimise acceptance of such lands, and for the papacy to
enjoy formal dominion over them, something more was required.
To this end Christophorous faked the 'Donation of Constantine'.

In it, 'Constantine recounts the legend [accepted as historical
fact in the eighth century] of his healing from leprosy during his
baptism by Pope Sylvester I. In gratitude for this miracle, and
in recognition of Sylvester's inheritance of the power of Peter to
bind and loose, Constantine sets the Pope and his successors for
ever above all other bishops and churches throughout the world.
He gives him also "all the prerogatives of our supreme imperial
position and the glory of our authority". Constantine tells how he
himself handed Sylvester his imperial crown ...'[6]

The document set out the territorial extent of the 'donation':

> In imitation of our own power, in order that for that cause the supreme
> pontificate may not deteriorate, but may rather be adorned with power
> and glory even more than is the dignity of an earthly rule: behold
> we—giving over to the oft—mentioned most blessed pontiff, our father
> Sylvester the universal pope, as well our palace, as has been said, as
> also the city of Rome and all the provinces, districts and cities of Italy
> or of the western regions; and relinquishing them, by our inviolable
> gift, to the power and sway of himself or the pontiffs his successors—do
> decree, by this our godlike charter and imperial constitution, that it
> shall be (so) arranged; and do concede that they (the palaces, provinces
> etc.) shall lawfully remain with the holy Roman church.[7]

History has been satisfied to point the finger at Christophorous for the fake, but the fact that he was an official of the papal court, and that the pope and the papacy would be prime beneficiaries of the forgery, would make it appear the guilt for the crime might go some way beyond the sole personage of Christophorous.

With the link between the Pope and the Emperor in Byzantium severed, and Rome in need of a strong protector, it was only a matter of time until a powerful new ruler was found to take the pope under his wing: Charlemagne. Son of Pepin the Short, Charlemagne ('Charles the Great', or 'Carolus Magnus') was brave, clever and energetic. He encouraged the arts and letters too, giving his name to the Carolingian Renaissance. He also became the first Holy Roman Emperor.

Charlemagne had succeeded his father (and brother) to the Frankish crown in 771, swiftly launching a northern campaign into Germany, pursuing territory and Christian converts. When the Vatican again appealed for help against the resurgent Lombards, he led his army over the Alps to subdue them, capturing Pavia in 774.

The external threat to Rome had subsided, but two decades later another pope would once again call upon the help of Charlemagne, this time following internal strife. Elected in 795, Pope Leo III had barely escaped the gouging out of his eyes and cutting off of his tongue by rivals who had accused him of sexual and other crimes. Asked to preside over the trial of the pope, Charlemagne went to Rome, but did not consider himself empowered to make such a judgement. Leo settled matters by swearing a solemn oath that he was not guilty, and arranged a public ceremony for his benefactor, the protector of Rome. The ceremony was in many ways an inverted reprise of the fanciful passing of the imperial crown from Constantine to Pope Sylvester.

'Two days later, during the third mass of Christmas, Leo picked up the imperial crown and placed it on Charlemagne's head while the crowd shouted out three times ... Then, for the first and last time in history, the pope knelt down before the new emperor in an act of homage. The Roman Empire, which came to be called the Holy Roman Empire, was re-established in Rome itself.'[8]

What had once been the single Roman Empire had become in effect two empires, the Greek and the Latin. The Byzantines, still adhering to the principle of unity, regarded the coronation of Charlemagne as an act of schism within the Empire. The creation of a Holy Roman Empire in the West, doctrinal differences, and acts of brutality committed by the Crusaders, only served to alienate east and west more than before, until eventually the Western Church and the Eastern Orthodox Church became separate churches in separate empires.

Although its name would later instil disdain in some such as Voltaire, the Holy Roman Empire survived for more than a thousand years—even outliving Voltaire himself[9]—until Napoleon brought down the curtain on it in 1804, defeating the last Emperor, Francis II.

✠ ✠ ✠

A century after Charlemagne's time, Rome was again deeply riven by factional chaos, the city paralysed as two syndicates battled for control of the papacy, its wealth and possessions. This time it was the factions of Formosus (pope 891–6) and the man who occupied the Throne of Saint Peter soon after his death, Stephen VI (896–7). The state of war between the two camps reached its nadir at the 'Synod Horrenda', otherwise called the 'Synod of the Cadaver', in early 897, at which the rotting corpse of the eight-month dead Formosus was put on 'trial' by Stephen.

'The corpse was provided with a counsel, who wisely kept silent while Pope Stephen raved and screamed his insults at it … The real crime of Formosus was that he had been a member of the opposite faction and had crowned 'emperor' one of the numerous illegitimate descendants of Charlemagne after having performed the same office for the candidate favoured by Pope Stephen's party.'[10]

On the grounds of this disagreement, and the various other pretexts for which his corpse had been dragged from its tomb and re-clad in papal robes, Formosus was duly found guilty and condemned. As the death sentence was no longer an option, Pope Stephen ordered the corpse to be stripped of its papal vestments, and the three now skeletal fingers of the right hand, once used for blessing, to be chopped off. The corpse was then dragged around the streets of Rome, no doubt as a public warning to those who still supported the faction of Formosus, before being tossed into the Tiber. The body was later recovered by fishermen, who re-buried it properly.

No such final dignity awaited Pope Stephen. The supporters of Formosus, unbowed by the ghastly display, rose against the pope and imprisoned him, before having him strangled just a few months after the notorious 'trial' he staged. That murder in turn led to virtual war on the streets of Rome. Years of chaos ensued, the papal office became a revolving door, with popes murdered and bloodshed rife.

'Stephen was followed by Romanus (897), who was deposed after four months and apparently imprisoned in a monastery. Theodore II (897) served for only 20 days, dying of natural causes, to be followed by John IX (898–900) who was pope for two years, while Benedict IV (900–03) managed three. Benedict may have been murdered, though that is not certain, but Leo V (903), who followed him certainly was. Leo was imprisoned by the priest Christopher who proclaimed himself (an anti) pope. He was then put to death, along with Christopher, by Sergius III (904–11).'[11]

For well over a century the Church and papacy would remain wracked with violence, murder and mutilation, with one pope in three dying in circumstances deemed suspicious.[12] But as the seven-year span of his papacy would suggest, Sergius brought at least some stability. He was backed by the Roman nobility, notably among them a duke with the Greek name of Theophylact, who came from the Etruscan town of Tusculum, to the southeast of Rome. Little is known about the duke himself, beyond his helping to maintain something approaching order during the years of factional mayhem and rebuilding the earthquake-damaged Lateran Palace, but his wife, Theodora, and two daughters, Marozia[13] and Theodora, are noted in the history of Rome and the papacy. Occasionally maligned as whores, the female Theophylacts were powerbrokers who for decades fashioned Rome and the Vatican in their own image. And from them too, it is thought, grew the legend of Pope Joan.

The main account of the Theophylact women survives from the bitter pen of a Lombard bishop called Liudprand, who wrote of them: 'A certain shameless strumpet called Theodora at one time was the sole monarch of Rome and—shame though it is to write it—exercised power like a man. She had two daughters, Marozia and Theodora, who were not only her equals but could surpass her in the exercises that Venus loves.'[14] Drawing upon this account, a Church historian in the sixteenth century coined the term 'pornocracy' for the ascendancy of the Theophylact women.

Various accounts attest that Marozia did have a sexual liaison with Pope Sergius, to whom she bore a son (who himself later became pope)—but many women have had sexual relations with popes and not been labelled whores as Liudprand painted the Theophylacts. Theodora effectively ruled through the desire of the Pope for her teenage daughter Marozia. After the death of Sergius in 911 and the two brief pontificates that followed his, she reinforced her authority by arranging the papacy for Archbishop John of Ravenna, a lover of the younger Theodora, Marozia's sister, a state of affairs bemoaned by Liudprand as 'O—monstrous crime!'. As Pope John X, this intimate of the Theophylacts would rule Rome and the Christian world for the next fourteen years, and for a time ensured abiding power and influence to the elder Theodora and her two daughters.

Marozia had meanwhile married a Tuscan warlord, Alberic, and borne him a son, also named Alberic—who as a young man would later intervene catastrophically in her affairs. Records become very sketchy at this point, but it appears a power struggle occurred between John X and the Theophylacts—and by the time it was over, Marozia's husband Alberic was dead, both Theodoras gone, and the sole figure of Marozia, now a powerful senatrix, was left facing her former ally the Pope.

Accounts of Marozia are few and lack detail, but some recount a 'tigress', a woman who was 'sensual, but capable of employing her beauty coldly as a political weapon; fierce, debauched, revengeful—but also highly competent, highly intelligent.'[15]

When Pope John attempted to assert his independence over Marozia's authority in Rome, a desperate power struggle broke out. The scales tilted Marozia's way when she married another feudal warlord, Guy of Provence. With his backing, Marozia had Pope John jailed in the Castel Sant'Angelo in 928, and smothered to death the following year. She then busied herself on behalf of her first son, John, the illegitimate son of Sergius, and following two short-lived pontificates she succeeded in having him installed as pope in 931: her son John XI was just 25 years old.

The following year, having got what she needed from Guy, she elected to marry his half-brother Hugh of Provence, a descendent of Charlemagne and putative king of Italy, and a man of renowned appetites. 'Hugh was the most accomplished satyr of his day, his royal court resembling a brothel at which Italians marvelled. But though Marozia was doubtless a powerful attraction for such a man, even stronger was the attraction of the dowry she would bring him … Unhesitatingly Hugh defamed his mother's memory, branding his half-brother bastard, and when another brother furiously protested, had his eyes dug out and imprisoned him.'[16]

The wedding of Hugh and Marozia in the Roman spring of 932 was to be a family affair, the nuptials presided over by the Pope, John XI, Marozia's illegitimate son by Pope Sergius. But as the nobility of Rome assembled for the ceremony, disaster struck. Fearing that he would become powerless under his new stepfather, a man who had already struck him in anger, Marozia's teenage son Alberic ran shouting through the streets of Rome, denouncing his own mother as a harlot and warning the people that they would be serfs of their new master from Provence.

'The Romans responded. It was as though Marozia has exerted a Circe-like spell upon them for nearly six years, reducing the most ferocious mob in history to an apathetic mass of slaves. Whatever the spell, it broke at that moment …'[17]

Marozia was abandoned by Hugh, who escaped the mobs by using a rope to lower himself down outside the city walls, and fled. Marozia's son Pope John XI was put under house arrest, and died four years later. Marozia herself was imprisoned for years, in some accounts decades, in the Castel Sant'Angelo, before her murder at the hands of her own grandson.[18]

The most likely explanation for the legend of 'Pope Joan' is a mingling of the story of Marozia, the woman who ran a papacy of Johns, with the popular tenth century tale of a young girl who through cleverness and guile becomes pope. 'There are many variants of her name. In some sources she is Agnes or Gilberta, but Joan is the most commonly used. According to the sources, this is because her papal name was John. The legends claim she was a brilliant woman, possibly English by birth, who disguised her gender in order to study in Athens, then came back to Rome where she rose through the papal civil service until she was elected pope. Joan's deception was discovered when, as she was making her way by horse between the Lateran and St Peter's, she gave birth to a child. A hysterical crowd had her dragged around the city tied to the horse's tail, and eventually stoned to death.'[19]

So flourished the legend of a 'Pope Joan', one which has come down to contemporary times, along with the equally popular tale that each new pope is asked to sit upon an open-bottomed throne like a commode and viewed from below to ensure that he is scrotally equipped to be God's Vicar on Earth.

3. THE HAIRSHIRT PONTIFF ON THE ROAD TO AVIGNON

In the country of the blind the one eyed man is king.

—ERASMUS

The fall of the Theophylacts in the eleventh century ushered in a period of somewhat less turbulent times, but in the late thirteenth century a corrosive power struggle between two of the oldest and the most influential families of Rome resulted in new paroxysms for the papal office.

The Orsini and Colonna families had been literally taking the Throne of Saint Peter in turns, when in 1294 the cardinals were deadlocked in electing the next pope. Support in the Conclave evenly divided between candidates from each family—and, more widely, loyalties to the Guelphs and Ghibellines[1]—with neither side able to secure the necessary two-thirds majority[2].

The Conclave had dragged on for more than two years, even being relocated to Perugia to escape the oppressive summer heat and an outbreak of plague in Rome. When still no candidate could be agreed upon, and with the citizenry demanding a decision—the practice had begun of bricking in the cardinals until they elected the next pope—a wild-card entry gained unanimous agreement from the exhausted cardinals. But in electing the illiterate[3] cave-dwelling mystic Pietro di Morrone[4] as their head, they had chosen the mediaeval equivalent of a hippie cult leader to be CEO of General Motors. Indeed, any modern cult leader would be better equipped to be a CEO than Morrone was for the papacy.

He was born into a peasant family in 1215 and became a Benedictine monk, but left the monastery for the mountain solitude of the Abruzzi, east of Rome. He lived a hermit's life of extreme privation in the mould of John the Baptist, as befitted a mystic anchorite[5] of the era, clad in a hairshirt and weighed down with iron chains, praying all day into the night, subsisting on little more than water and crusts of dry bread. Given his diet, or lack thereof, it is not surprising he began experiencing visions, which ultimately brought fame from far afield to the cave-dwelling holy man. He founded his own order devoted to the Holy Ghost, which became known as the Celestines, and to escape the ever-increasing traffic of pilgrims, retreated to a cave at the hermitage of San Onofrio, on another remote peak.

But even thence his fame spread, attracting the eye of the French king of Naples, Charles II of Anjou, who made the difficult journey to meet him in 1293, and devised a plan which was to have serious consequences for the Church for many decades to come. Charles encouraged the holy hermit to write a letter to the cardinals criticising them for their drawn-out deliberations. Their snap response, which the king might well have anticipated from such exhausted and frazzled men, was to elect Pietro himself.

The vote taken, the pope-elect had to be advised of his elevation to the pontificate, which meant dispatching Vatican envoys on a journey of some 200 kilometres to the remote and rugged mountains where the elderly hermit resided. Clad in their Vatican finery, the envoys were joined en route on this curious expedition by a throng of monks and other faithful, ultimately scrabbling up the rocks to the hermit's lofty refuge, '... a cave over a thousand feet up on the desolate mountain. It was set upon a narrow plateau, with a sheer drop upon one side, and there the party was forced to crowd. News of the approaching cortege had filled Peter [Pietro] not so much with dismay as outright terror. He had intended to fly yet again to one of his remoter refuges, but his disciples, with a keener awareness of the fruits involved, had dissuaded him. When (met) he was peering out through the bars of his cell, his eyelids swollen and darkened by tears, his face emaciated. He barely seemed to understand what was being said to him; then he threw himself upon the ground, prayed, arose, and with infinite reluctance, accepted.'[6]

By the time Pietro and his entourage descended the mountain, the joyful word of a new pope at last had spread far and wide, and a cheering multitude estimated in the hundreds of thousands poured in to greet the startled pontiff-elect. The next surprise for all concerned was that the new pontiff did not wish to go to Rome to be crowned, but accepted an invitation from King Charles to go south to Naples, where the unhappy cardinals eventually agreed to join him. In Naples Pietro di Morrone established his papacy as Celestine V.

From the outset things were difficult. The new pope chose to live humbly in a custom-built replica of his mountain cell, and could not speak Latin, the language of the papal court, but vernacular Italian, the roughness of which assaulted the delicate ears of the papal courtiers. He also appeared to have little idea of his role and his power to rule by decree, and from the outset dispensed positions and money virtually to anyone who bothered to ask, and inevitably they were great in number.

This became most serious and had the longest-lasting and most deleterious effects, when at the request of his French patron Charles, Pietro ordained eight new French cardinals, drastically shifting the balance of power in the cardinalate towards France.

For the time being, however, the faithful rejoiced at the elevation of a bona-fide hairshirt holy man, dancing for joy in a much anticipated mediaeval-style 'Summer of Love'. 'The election of a simple good man, who was taken from his cave to mount the most splendid throne in Europe, had first astonished and then delighted Christians. It seemed as though they were witnessing the working out of those recent prophecies which foretold a new dispensation, when the meek would rule the mighty …'[7]

It was not to be, all unravelling with frightening speed. 'In a little over a month, Celestine reduced the bureaucracy to chaos with his casual gifts and retractions creating an inextricable tangle … Celestine was in an impossible position. On one side were the men to whom he had given a new order and hope, exhorting him to begin the reign of love. On another were the tough and cynical papal bureaucrats who were either employing him for their own ends or were attempting to force his whole way of life into an alien mould.'[8]

The cardinals knew something had to be done, but what? Depose him, with such passionate popular support, not to mention that of his landlord and patron, the powerful Neapolitan king? Impossible. Then one of their number, Cardinal Benedetto Caetani, realising Pietro was as uncomfortable with the papacy as it was with him, came up with an unprecedented plan, apparently without the knowledge of the other cardinals, and presented it to the hermit pope.

On 13 December 1294, only four months after his coronation, a trembling Pietro resigned his office before the stunned assembly of cardinals, and then, divesting himself of his papal robes before their startled eyes and re-donning his hairshirt, walked out. All eyes then turned to the man who had composed the resignation, Cardinal Caetani. Despite deep rumblings over the legality and circumstances of what had occurred by his hand, nine days later the cardinals reconvened and this time took just one day to elect Caetani himself, who took the name Boniface VIII.

Fearing opposition could coalesce around the abdicated pope and question his legitimacy, the new pontiff took the hermit into his company on the journey back north, but the old man was not for Rome and absconded, rejoining his followers in the mountains, to much rejoicing. When Boniface ordered him arrested, Pietro slipped through his fingers again, becoming a shadowy itinerant in the Italian countryside, until he was captured attempting to gain passage across the Adriatic to Greece. He spent three years in prison, badly treated, until Boniface had him murdered in his cell. So ended the life of a simple man who yearned for solitude but was dragged into the machinery of Rome against his will, crushed and spat out. The sole consolation for his followers was his canonisation in 1313, less than two decades after his death.

The man who had presided over the hermit's murder would have been well aware of the monstrousness of his own actions. Benedetto Caetani (1235–1303) was an experienced jurist with long experience as a papal legate abroad. Born into an aristocratic family in Anagni, outside Rome, he studied canon law in Spoleto and Bologna before entering the papal service. His legal knowledge proved a boon to the Vatican, and he was dispatched on important diplomatic missions to France and England before being promoted to the rank of cardinal in 1291. Although he maintained a studied neutrality during the two year deadlock between the Orsini and Colonna that had eventually resulted in the election of Celestine V, he was still suspected by each side of secretly supporting the other. His brutal conflict later with the Colonna only served to confirm their own worst suspicions, and pushed them into the camp of France's king, Philip the Fair.

Boniface and Philip fell out in 1296 over the levying of taxes upon the Church and its clergy, money which Philip said he needed for his ongoing war with England. The situation was exacerbated the following year after a mule train laden with gold bound for the Vatican was robbed by the men of two Colonna cardinals. When Boniface demanded his gold back, the two cardinals refused. In the ensuing months, mobs sacked the palaces of the Colonna, with ready absolution from the pope, who ultimately declared a 'crusade' against the powerful family. Their allies, even their serfs, were killed and enslaved, farms and ancient olive groves put to the torch. In a single shameful act, one of the sacred monuments of the Roman world was razed to the ground upon the orders of Boniface, the ancient town of Palestrina.

'It was an act without precedent in papal history. Palestrina was one of the seven pillars of the Roman Church, for it had been the seat of a bishop from the remotest days. Its monuments dated back to the days of imperial Rome, protected by the Colonna, whose family seat was the great palace supposed to have been built by Julius Caesar himself. The family had gathered within the walls those treasures of the past which their contemporaries despised or ignored, making the city a priceless museum. Boniface did not

intend the usual token destruction—the demolition of a section or
wall or a tower or two—but the total eradication of one of the ancient
cities of Italy.'[9] Boniface went further than razing the city to the
ground, literally salting the wound of the Colonna by pouring salt
in the fields to kill any further cultivation, as the Romans had done
after the sack of ancient Carthage.[10]

Not surprisingly, the Colonna went to Philip the Fair to
see how they could help him in his conflict with the Pope. Their
cause was joined by the new leader of the Celestine Order, the
reconstructed rake, poet and tragic widower Jacopone da Todi,
who like many among the populace of Italy considered Boniface's
pontificate utterly illegal, and agitated against him.

Although he was well aware of all the countervailing currents,
Boniface continued on his way with full papal pomp and ceremony.
This reached its climax in his proclamation of the year 1300 as
a Jubilee Year, in which he 'called all Christians to embark not
on a crusade to the holy land but a pilgrimage to Rome that
would earn them plenary indulgences that would release them
from punishment for sins. During 1300, as many as two million
Christians journeyed to Rome.'[11]

Centrestage at this grand Roman expo stood Boniface VIII
himself, robed in magnificence with arms open wide to his millions
of followers. Yet, as so often happens, from this proud zenith he
would promptly tumble into ignominy.

The imbroglio with Philip over taxation was brought to a
head in 1301 with the arrest of Bishop Bernard Saisset of Pamiers
in France on charges of sedition. By demanding that the king try
his bishop in a clerical court, Boniface directly challenged the
legal jurisdiction of the French monarch. Boniface followed with
the bull *Unam Sanctam*, 'the clearest and probably the most logical
statement concerning the temporal sovereignty of popes ever

made.'[12] In asserting the primacy of the 'one Holy Church', and noting 'if the secular power strays from the way, it shall be judged by the spiritual', it left the crowned heads of Christendom in little doubt about whom Pope Boniface considered held ultimate power. As such, it was an open challenge to Philip the Fair.

'It was the clarity of the statement that made it impressive, leaving no room for doubt or casuistry: and the fact that, without even mentioning him, it publicly condemned the most powerful king in Europe.'[13] The French response was a public assault on the character of the Pope, culminating in a dossier compiled by Philip's councillor Guillaume de Nogaret, with assistance from the Colonna and Jacopone da Todi.

'The real force of Nogaret's indictment was to consist in repugnant and obscene personal slanders on Boniface, culled from the tittle-tattle of the streets in Italy. This was calculated to achieve its effect by sheer weight of denigration. There were stories that Boniface was an unbeliever; a Sodomite; a dealer in magic. Repulsive little tales about the procuring of women and advances made to bootboys would have left little shred of dignity about Boniface, if he had lived to hear them alleged against him in a public trial.'[14]

Philip conspired to bring the Pope before just such a trial. In September 1303 French forces linked up with men of the Colonna family and moved against Boniface, then sick in bed in his palace, in his home town of Anagni. The ailing pope was seized by the intruders, but the alarm was raised and he was delivered from their hands, the agents fleeing back to France. The attack prompted outrage in Rome.

'The violent attack on Boniface VIII by French troops who invaded the papal palace at Anagni in 1303 was a staggering reversal of the collaboration between the popes and the kings of France which had been a steady force in European politics for nearly two centuries.'[15]

Despite the failure of the plot, the French king's audacious action had at a stroke inverted *Unam Sanctam*, and demonstrated it to be merely words on a page. The pope did not possess temporal power over kings; rather, it was very much vice versa.

Boniface died in Rome a few weeks after the attempted abduction. And now the threads of what had occurred during the bizarre election of Celestine V—itself the product of the seemingly endless rivalry between the Colonna and Orsini—drew together fatally when the French cardinals whom Celestine had appointed at the request of his French host, Charles II of Naples, ensured a majority for the Frenchman Raymond Bertrand de Got in the Conclave of 1305.[16]

As Clement V, the new French pope moved decisively to enforce French and personal control of the cardinalate and the Church. 'Shortly after his coronation Clement created ten new cardinals, of whom nine were French—and four of these were his nephews.'[17]

Clement formalised French authority over the papal tiara four years later when in 1309 he moved the papal seat itself to Avignon, in the south of France. The Church was truly now a house divided, between Avignon and Rome, between French and Italians, and for seven chaotic decades the Church was hostage to Avignon popes and Roman popes, popes who claimed legitimacy and antipopes with little claim or none.

Though himself French-born, Pope Gregory XI returned the papacy to Rome in January 1377, where he died the following year, and when the cardinals convened they elected a Neapolitan Italian, Bartolomeo Prignano, Pope Urban IV. Not that his election ended the troubles—they continued on as before, unabated.

'Urban IV's harsh criticism of the cardinals led to the Great Western Schism, with two different popes vying for the support of European powers. Urban quarrelled with his army and his allies and it is possible he met his death by poisoning.'[18]

The fourteenth century saw seemingly endless troubles, characterised most tellingly by the Hundred Years War and the ravages of the Plague,[19] but for the Church at least the papacy was restored to Rome, the bridge of Avignon crossed.[20]

4. HIT FOR SIXTUS: THE PAPAL PATSY

> How passing fair is youth,
> Forever fleeting away.
>
> —LORENZO DE' MEDICI

On Easter Sunday in 1478, the good burghers of Florence gathered in the Duomo, the splendid cathedral which sits at the heart of their equally splendid city, to celebrate the traditional High Mass marking the miraculous resurrection of Jesus Christ from his tomb. Amidst the hundreds crowding the pews that day were the young Medici brothers, Lorenzo, not yet thirty years of age and ruler of Florence, and Giuliano. Among the other worshippers in the Duomo was a priest named Francesco de' Pazzi, who intended to lead the assassinations of the brothers in a coup d'etat to end Medici rule of the Florentine Republic. Before the sun set that day, the River Arno ran red with the blood of the dead.

Francesco's family, the Pazzi, had grievances against the Medici going back generations to when Giovanni de' Medici, the great grandfather of Lorenzo and Giuliano and founder of the banking dynasty, had imposed taxes on the rich to the benefit of the poor. The move had predictably made Giovanni de' Medici popular on the street but detested in the halls of the aristocracy. Since then the Pazzi had watched the seemingly irrevocable rise of the House of Medici, through Cosimo ('The Wise') and his son Piero, to Lorenzo. The young Lorenzo was a popular ruler, gifted and outgoing, able to handle himself in a joust, but also a composer of lyrical poetry and songs. In other words, he was just the man to make Pazzi blood boil.

The Pazzi had long nursed the ambition of bringing down the Medici, and it was via the scheming of a pope, Sixtus IV, that they almost achieved their aim, although in truth the Pope played the Pazzi for a patsy.

Sixtus IV was born Francesco della Rovere near Savona, in Liguria. He joined the Franciscan Order and ascended the ranks to become its head in 1464, and a cardinal three years later. He was elected pope in 1471, and promptly addressed himself to temporal problems by dispatching a fleet against the Turks at Smyrna, an assault which failed dismally. In addition to his public works—he is remembered as an energetic engineer of roads, bridges and aqueducts—Sixtus IV joined a long line of papal nepotists. He installed his relatives into key Church positions while scheming with them to expand the Papal States, but the now infamous Pazzi Conspiracy became his most notorious exploit.

The plot was hatched between the Pope's nephew Girolamo Riario and Francesco de' Pazzi, then in self-imposed exile from Florence, after the two young men met in Rome. The plan approved by Sixtus was to overthrow the Medici and turn the prized Florentine republic into a papal fiefdom under Girolamo, effectively annexing it to the Papal States. The scheme was supported by Jacopo, head of the House of Pazzi. It appealed to the

Pazzis on many counts, especially in humiliating the insufferable Medici, but for Sixtus it promised a massive boost to his coffers. Florence was a commercial dynamo, grown rich on the fabric trade and banking. After decades under the Medici, among the most powerful banking families in Europe, Florence was literally stuffed with riches in gold and jewels, fabrics and furnishings, artworks and rare and treasured books.

To Sixtus, it was a fat plum ripe on the branch, but it was well fortified and defended. Through the Pazzi, with their long-standing grievances and aristocratic pretensions, he glimpsed a means to take the city-state from within, in a coup: the Pazzi were just the men to pluck the plum for him.

The plotters saw their first opportunity to strike at a banquet given by Lorenzo on 25 April 1478 at his villa in the hills of Fiesole outside Florence, but because Lorenzo's brother Giuliano was ill and unable to attend, the plan was postponed until the next day, Easter Sunday. Even then it was uncertain whether Giuliano would be able to attend, but because of its importance in the Christian calendar, special arrangements were made to get him there.

Francesco de' Pazzi took his place in the pew behind the two Medici brothers, and gripped the dagger concealed in his priestly garb. He had chosen the dramatic high-point in the mass as his moment to strike, and when the officiating cardinal raised the Sacred Host high, the bells rang and the congregation all bowed their heads, he leapt forward and thrust his dagger into the unsuspecting Giuliano, following up the first strike with a furious assault until the young man lay mortally wounded on the marble floor of the cathedral, bleeding from twenty stab wounds. Lorenzo had also been attacked by Francesco's accomplices, but here the murderous coup went awry. Although injured and bleeding from a serious stab wound to the neck, Lorenzo managed to fend off his would-be assassins and escape with his supporters to safety.

By this time the Duomo was in uproar and confusion, with Giuliano lying dead, others, including Francesco bleeding from wounds, and the gentlewomen of Florence weeping over their fallen menfolk while the fight raged on around them. The chaos soon spread to the streets and piazzas as the extent of the conspiracy became apparent.

As planned, an ally of the Pope and the Pazzi, Archbishop Salviati of Pisa, had tried to take control of the government, believing the two Medici brothers successfully murdered. But as word got out that Lorenzo had survived, the people turned upon Salviati and hanged him from a window of the palace. The Pazzi clan then attempted to take control of the streets by force of arms, trying to rally the people to their cause with a cry of 'Liberty!', but they received scant support, and confronted by a throng of citizens loyal to the Medici and the republic, took flight.

In the bloodbath that followed, more than two hundred members of the Pazzi, Papal allies, and others even conceivably connected with the plot, were killed, including Jacopo, head of the House of Pazzi, whose mutilated corpse was dragged through the streets. Francesco de' Pazzi, killer of Giuliano Medici, finished up at the end of a rope beside Archbishop Salviati. Other members of the Pazzi clan were beheaded. The man who stood to gain most from the coup, Sixtus IV, was the only conspirator to escape its collapse virtually unscathed. But instead of any penitence for the plot and the loss of life, and in spite of irrefutable evidence linking him with it, the pontiff went on the attack.

'Infuriated by the failure of the plot, the Pope demanded that Lorenzo surrender and that the Florentine government answer before an ecclesiastical court ... The sovereigns of Europe sided with the Medici; the Pope excommunicated the Florentine state;

the Florentine clergy outlawed him in turn; the Pope declared war.'[1] Hostilities failed to amount to much after the declaration, largely because the Pope had a much more pressing threat to deal with in a Turkish incursion into southern Italy.

The Pazzi conspiracy did have an abiding effect on Rome in one respect, however, through the murdered Giuliano de' Medici. As was the custom with young nobles, he had been liberally sewing his wild oats, and a pretty young Florentine girl had borne him a son named Giulio. Grief-stricken over the death of his brother, Lorenzo was determined to locate the infant, illegitimate or not.'It was not a difficult task in a city of a hundred thousand people; nor had the girl been at pains to conceal the illustrious parentage of her child. She made no difficulties about passing her son over to the lord of Florence and Lorenzo brought up the child as his own.'[2]

Chastened and more vigilant after the failed plot, Lorenzo lived another decade and a half, becoming a statesman and patron of the arts. 'The lover of art and letters more than maintained the fame of his family—he increased it by his boundless liberality. Under his enlightened lead Florence became the mother of arts and the cultural capital of Italy, imitated but unsurpassed by other states. He set the pace, the other princes were compelled to compete; but he was the highest bidder for the services of scholars and artists and carried off all the prizes for the glory of Florence and the greater glory of the Medici.'[3]

He became known as Lorenzo the Magnificent, in time followed by two Medici popes, Lorenzo's own son Giovanni, who would become Leo X, and Giulio, the illegitimate son of Giuliano, who would become Pope Clement VII.

As for Sixtus IV, he lasted six years after the failed plot, built the Sistine Chapel which bears his name, became a patron of artists such as Botticelli—who among others painted frescoes for the Sistine walls—condemned the worst excesses of the Spanish Inquisition, and even established a refuge for orphans. But it is for his attempted bloody coup against the Medici, and his Chapel, that he is most remembered.

5. BORGIA, THE PAPAL BULL

One can make this generalisation about men: they are ungrateful,
fickle, liars, and deceivers, they shun danger and are
greedy for profit.

—MACHIAVELLI, *THE PRINCE*

S uch was the impact of the Borgias upon the world of the Renaissance that their name still retains its power to evoke thoughts of treachery, debauchery and murder. The head of the Borgia clan was something else too: a pope. The Roman Catholic Church has long sighed with resignation about its numerous 'bad popes', but to many eyes Pope Alexander VI, Rodrigo Borgia, was the baddest of the bad, bad to the bone. Whether this is the truth is still a matter of debate among mediaeval historians, where reputations have been forged by the latest revision upwards of his reputation, or a freshly penned scathing rebuttal.

It is fitting that the coat of arms of the Borgia family is a bull: Rodrigo Borgia was the bull in the china shop of the Vatican. He lived with faint regard to the moral code of his Church or his times, wielded papal authority like a grasping duke, and instilled fear into friend and foe alike, a practice refined into an art form by his even more notorious son, Cesare, upon whose statecraft of cynicism, or realpolitik, Niccolo Machiavelli in part, at the least, wrought *The Prince*. Accounts of Cesare's sister Lucrezia as a seductress and poisoner, a definitive femme fatale, have also spiced the pages of history and popular fiction.

The first hurdle Rodrigo Borgia had to cross on his way to the Church's highest office, was that he was a Spaniard. He was born in Valencia in 1531, but the ambitious young cleric was fortunate to arrive in Rome under the patronage of a fellow Borgia, his uncle Pope Calixtus III, who later made him a cardinal. Calixtus also brought Rodrigo's elder brother Pedro to Rome. He invested him with titles, but Pedro's avarice for the gold of the leading families of Rome eventually brought about his downfall, and he died in exile.

At the age of 30, after Rodrigo had already fathered three children with various mistresses, he took a Roman aristocrat, Vanozza dei Cataneis, as his lover. It would prove no mere fling: they remained together for more than a quarter of a century, and she bore him four children, including Cesare and Lucrezia.[1]

It is said of the sometimes jovial but often querulous and endlessly scheming Rodrigo, that at least he loved his family, as he certainly did. Eventually, however, he took the younger and more glamorous Giulia Farnese as his mistress, when he was in his fifties and approaching the apogee of his power.

Rodrigo made little attempt to mask his worldly appetites and, on the contrary, so flaunted them as a rising young cardinal that Pope Pius II had cause to chastise him severely.

'Beloved Son, We have heard that, four days ago, several ladies of Siena—women entirely given over to worldly frivolities—were assembled in the gardens of the Giovanni di Bichis ... We have heard that the most licentious dances were indulged in, none of the allurements of love were lacking and you conducted yourself in a wholly worldly manner. Shame forbids mention of all that took place—not only the acts themselves but their very names are unworthy of your position ... All Siena is talking about this orgy ...'[2]

Despite such admonishments, Rodrigo Borgia maintained a steady march upwards through the Church hierarchy, and when Pope Innocent VIII died in 1492, he considered the papal tiara itself within his grasp. By then he was one of the most experienced operators in the Vatican, and only too aware the votes of the Conclave of Cardinals were open to the highest bidder. He had amassed a fortune from his offices in the Church, and was determined to outbid his Italian rivals for the prize.

'His revenues from his papal offices, his abbeys in Italy and Spain, and his three bishoprics are vast. His office of Vice Chancellor alone yields him 8000 gold ducats annually. His plate, his pearls, his stuffs embroidered with silk and gold, his books are all of such high quality as would befit a king or pope. Altogether it is believed that he possesses more gold and riches of every sort than all the other cardinals put together.'[3]

The Conclave reached an easy decision in his favour, the smoke poured from the chimneys of the Vatican announcing his election, and unlikely as it might have appeared to powerbrokers in the years before, the sexagenarian Spaniard had won the papal prize. As such he was the best pope money could buy, even if later events revealed the unsatisfactory quality of the goods.

This is not to say that he did not possess personal virtues, or was unable at least to conjure the outline of them. As his official secretary remarked: 'He knew how to dominate, how to shine in conversation, how to appear dignified. Majestic in stature, he had the advantage over lesser men. He was just at that age, sixty, at which

Aristotle says men are wisest. He was robust in body and vigorous in mind and so was perfectly suited to his new position.'[4]

Not all who dealt with him were so easily charmed. The Florentine scholar Francesco Guicciardini wrote: 'His manner was dissolute. He knew neither shame nor sincerity, neither faith nor religion. Moreover he was possessed by an insatiable greed, and overwhelming ambition and a burning passion for the advancement of his many children who, in order to carry out his iniquitous decrees, did not scruple to employ the most heinous means.'[5]

Rodrigo Borgia had, however, inherited a papacy already diminished by many years of profligate and scandalous behaviour: 'the corruption, which seemed to culminate in this family, was already far advanced when they came to Rome.'[6]

As such it was not their notorious personal behaviour which would bring abiding opprobrium to the house of Borgia, but their methods of achieving their ends, a melding of terror and treachery later proclaimed the ideal for rulers by Machiavelli. 'Their [the Borgias] immediate purpose, which in fact, they attained, was the complete subjugation of the Pontifical State.'[7]

To bolster his authority, on assuming the papacy Alexander made his son Cesare a cardinal, even if the young man had limited training and even less interest in clerical matters. He also schemed to break marriage vows exchanged on behalf of his teenage daughter Lucrezia with a Spanish dynasty of no further use to him, betrothing her to Giovanni Sforza, an Italian prince of promise and influence, lord of Pesaro and kin to the rulers of Milan.

Giovanni and Lucrezia were married with great pomp in the Vatican in 1493, the year after Alexander's accession. The marriage was not fated to last long, however. When shifting allegiances rendered the Sforzas of little more use, the young Giovanni was compelled to sign a statement that he was impotent and the marriage to Lucrezia unconsummated, and Alexander annulled the union. After the marriage was dissolved and while she was staying in a convent, Lucrezia became pregnant to an emissary sent by her father, but this detail did not prevent him issuing a bull declaring her a virgin. Such brazen behaviour had tongues wagging in Rome, and up and down the boot of Italy.

> *Throughout his papacy ... Alexander VI was surrounded by a buzz of scandal. Gossiping about popes has always been a favourite Italian pastime, but probably no other pope has ever afforded so much occasion for juicy gossip. Other popes had kept mistresses in the Vatican, and simony and immorality were no more rife in Rome under the Borgia Pope than they had been under his predecessors and would be under his successors. But there was a sort of childlike shamelessness about Alexander VI which invited comment. Other popes had auctioned off high ecclesiastical offices, doublecrossed their associates and allies, and used their exalted position for the advancement of their families and base personal ends, but usually they pretended to be doing something else. Rodrigo Borgia had either an honest scorn for hypocrisy or a naive ignorance of the force of public opinion. Other popes had thrown wild parties at the Vatican, but no other pope had made the parties so flamboyant or public. And no other pope had had a portrait of his official mistress, robed as the Virgin Mary, painted over the door of his bedchamber.*[8]

In this respect, at least, he did break new ground for sexual shenanigans in the Vatican. But ironically enough, although he was a career womaniser and his official mistress had numerous rivals, Alexander was in some other respects quite abstemious, and despite his corporeal bulk more sparing than some with food and drink. He is also considered to have acquitted himself as an able if not conscientious administrator, determined to make the Roman streets safer, and to trim the Vatican's notorious reels of red tape, as well as being something of a patron of the arts.

But it was his carnal activities which inevitably aroused the keenest interest, and soon after he took the papal throne the rumours spread of wild parties and orgies in the Vatican, even private bullfights in the courtyards. Some accused him of treating the Vatican as a high-class brothel. The rude Spaniards aroused the ire of the old ruling families of Rome, who despite any activities of their own demanded at least a degree of decorum. There was even talk of incest between the Borgias, chatter in part instigated and fanned along by powerful rivals and jilted former allies. All this led to agitation at home and abroad by Alexander's most bitter enemy, Cardinal Giuliano della Rovere, but it was an allegation of collusion by Alexander with the Muslim Sultan Bazajet that prompted the young French king, Charles VIII, to the view that the Borgia pope was a traitor to Christendom. A French invasion of the Italian peninsula followed.

The powerful French army met little resistance as it swept south. Charles and his men were welcomed into Florence by the preacher Girolamo Savonarola, who saw in Charles 'the sword of God' he had prophesied, and with French help he overthrew the ruling Medici and installed himself as Florentine ruler. Charles continued south, and entered Rome unopposed. As the new year 1495 dawned, his troops controlled the city and his advisors urged him to depose Alexander at once. But the young king was unsure of how to proceed.

'Once more the vast, undefinable, intangible power of the supreme pontiff and universal pope came to the aid of the Italian prince ... could the rest of Christendom be persuaded that they were acting from love of the Holy Church and not from plain politics? How would Charles's deeply religious subjects take it? And in any case, who would fill the vacant throne? In the last analysis, the decision was Charles's—a decision which the weak young man did not dare to make.'[9]

Instead of overthrowing the Pope, he exacted favours and, taking Alexander's son Cesare as a hostage, continued south to threaten the kingdom of Naples, to which he asserted a family claim. Cesare escaped and returned to Rome and although the French took Naples with little effort and indulged themselves in extended looting of its treasures, the entire campaign turned to sand in Charles's fingers. While he entertained himself in Naples, Alexander organised the powerful Venetians and Milanese, with support from Spain, into the coalition of the Holy League.

By the time Charles returned north he found himself pitted against very powerful forces, fighting every step of the way. The French saw their Neapolitan booty eaten away bit by bit, spent on sorely needed provisions and arms, and turned to ashes on the battlefield. In Florence, Charles's erstwhile friend Savonarola castigated him, saying he was incurring the wrath of God because he had failed in his holy duty to reform Rome. The climax came in July 1495, when troops of the Holy League vanquished the French in the Battle of Fornuovo near Parma in northern Italy. Charles lost nearly all his remaining loot, and the French straggled home across the Alps a harried, battered force.

Having dealt with Charles, Alexander now turned his attention to the problem of Florence itself, and the outspoken friar whose name he had added to his death list. Savonarola was born into the aristocracy and entered the Dominican Order, rising to become Vicar-General in 1493. As word filtered back from Rome about the excesses of newly installed Alexander, Savonarola started preaching fire and brimstone sermons against Christendom's moral decline, sexual licentiousness, corruption and the luxuries of earthly wealth.

He also spoke out against Florence's ruler, the now ailing Lorenzo de' Medici, although his words may also have been double-pointed, simultaneously aimed at Rome. 'Tyrants are incorrigible because they are proud, because they love flattery, because they will not restore their ill-gotten gains. They allow bad officials to have their way; they yield to adulation; they neither heed the poor nor condemn the rich ...'[10]

After the arrival of the French army and his usurpation of Medici power, Savonarola became in effect head of his own theocratic state, the so-called Catholic Commonwealth, backed by followers called the Piagnoni, the 'Weepers' or 'Snivellers', so named for the emotional reaction he elicited from them through his sermons. Savonarola sought to purge the wealthy city of Florence of its treasure trove of earthly finery, which went up in flames in his infamous Bonfire of the Vanities.

Although more than one such bonfire took place—and there had been previous instances of similar events in other parts of Italy—the most famous occurred at the onset of Lent in February 1497, when Savonarola sent his minions around the city collecting books and works of art, women's dresses and jewellery, cosmetics and mirrors, gambling tables, even chess sets, which were put to the torch on bonfires in the Piazza della Signoria.[11]

The Bonfires of the Vanities are believed to have devoured some fine Renaissance works during the fifteenth century, including some by the young Michelangelo Buonarroti. There were even accounts of young artists, among them Botticelli, a follower of Savonarola, becoming swept up in the fervour and tossing their own works onto the pyres.

Although Savonarola loathed Alexander and largely ignored his edicts from Rome, the friar's claims to the gift of prophecy led to an investigation of heresy in Florence, and he was forbidden to preach. His end came when the apocalypse he had predicted failed to eventuate, and a populace once urged to destroy its most precious possessions rioted a few months later, in May 1497. Drinking, gambling and bawdy behaviour spread through the city. With calls to restore the Medici, Savonarola's reign was effectively over.

Alexander had the last word against his enemy when he signed his death warrant in 1498. Savonarola and two of his disciples were strangled and burned in the Piazza della Signoria, where his infamous bonfire had burned only a year before.

✢ ✢ ✢

Alexander had little time to gloat on his triumph over Savonarola, however; he was stunned by the murder of his beloved eldest son Juan, the Duke of Gandia. Juan's corpse had been dragged from the Tiber the morning after a Borgia family dinner in the summer of 1497. The young man had been stabbed repeatedly. Theft was ruled out as a motive, as Juan's purse with a large sum in gold was found on the body. Although the identity of the killer was not confirmed, suspicion passed between a number of those who knew him, before settling upon his younger brother Cesare, the last person with whom Juan had been seen alive.

The Pope himself is said to have suspected Cesare of the fratricide, but out of fear of his own calculating and ruthless son, did nothing. 'Alexander was forced to acquiesce in the murder of his best-loved son, the Duke of Gandia [Juan], since he himself lived in hourly dread of Cesare.'[12]

Worse in many ways for Alexander, he now needed Cesare. He had preferred Juan to the younger Cesare, who, resenting a perceived lack of paternal affection, presented himself as cool and aloof, habitually dressed all in black. Now the ageing Pope had little choice but to turn to Cesare, whose diplomatic and military skills had already been shown, and upon whose practised brutality he would increasingly come to rely.

Dispatched as Alexander's envoy to the newly crowned Louis XII of France, Cesare capped the success of his mission by his marriage to Charlotte d'Albret, sister of the King of Navarre and daughter of the Duke of Guyenne. In the process he gained the Duchy of Valentinois, becoming Cesare Borgia of France, and known throughout Italy as Duke Valentino. His close relationship with Louis XII allowed Cesare to muster French troops for a scheme he and his father had hatched, to consolidate the Papal States in a military campaign through the cities of central Italy.

At the close of the fifteenth century, the Papal States were hemmed in by powerful neighbours—Venice, Naples, Milan, and France itself—as well as by prosperous city-states such as Florence and Bologna. But there was a jigsaw of smaller cities and principalities to Rome's north and south. These were held by the petty princes of the Italian nobility, and it was to bolster their strategic position that the Borgias, with the aid of French troops sent by Louis, set about reinforcing the Papal States by creating the neighbouring state of Romagna.

Cesare's campaign, akin to a fifteenth century blitzkrieg, saw forced marches and surprise attacks, with city after city besieged and falling. Some fell without a fight due to Cesare's famous skills at negotiation and his vaunted military might, and in fear of the consequences of doing otherwise. Those who did resist, such as the imperious and cultured Caterina Sforza in Forli, saw their battlements breached and treasuries plundered. Cesare is said to have raped the captive Caterina and kept her as a concubine until she managed to escape his clutches and flee.

His victories became the stuff of terrifying legend. After the fall of the city of Capua, where Cesare led the final attack on horseback, its citizenry were raped and butchered in the streets. 'Women, as usual, suffered the most with the inevitable rape preceding murder. Thirty of the most beautiful were captured and sent to Rome, Christians sent to the seat of Christendom as though to the court of a pagan prince. It was a Frenchman who recorded this incident, leaving it to Italian writers to elaborate it into a Herculean myth whereby Cesare took the women into his personal harem.'[13]

By now, Alexander and Cesare had decided that Lucrezia's second marriage to a Neapolitan noble, Alfonso, Duke of Bisceglie, was inconvenient for their alliance with France. In the midsummer of the year 1500 Alfonso was attacked and stabbed on the steps of Saint Peter's Basilica and left to die. One eyewitness reported the assailant was Cesare Borgia. When a few days later Alfonso was strangled in his bed, the task was said to have been done by Cesare's chief fixer, Don Michelotto, although other accounts had Cesare attending personally to his brother-in-law. Lucrezia had apparently loved her second husband, but this carried no weight with her father and brother. After a time of mourning, during which Cesare paid her close fraternal attention, Lucrezia was deemed adequately recovered for her next assignment, marriage to Alfonso D'Este, the powerful Duke of Ferrara, whom she wed in 1501.

By now the mere mention of the 'satanic' Cesare was enough to freeze hearts up and down Italy. 'The manner in which Cesare isolated his father, murdering brother, brother-in-law and other relations or courtiers whenever their favour with the Pope or their position in any other respect became inconvenient to him, is literally appalling.'[14]

The plans of Cesare and Alexander for the Romagna suffered a severe setback in 1502 with the Revolt of the Condottieri, the warlords and mercenaries of Cesare's campaign of conquest. Hearing rumours of a possible weakening of the French king's allegiance to Cesare, and that perhaps their master might not much longer be the force he had been, the *condottieri* conducted their own 'freelance' assault upon Bologna, which embarrassed Cesare and eventually brought him into direct conflict with many of his long-time comrades in arms.

The young Niccolo Machiavelli, Secretary of State of the Florentine Republic, had by then spent considerable time with Cesare and, liking what he saw, joined his campaign in October of 1502, becoming an eyewitness to the vanquishing of the *condottieri*. The author of *The Prince*, the little handbook of treachery traditionally said to be inspired by Satan (though inspired at least in part by Cesare Borgia), was described by a contemporary as:

> *Of middle height, slender figure, sparkling eyes, dark hair, rather a small head, a slightly aquiline nose, a tightly closed mouth; all about him bore the impress of a very acute observer and thinker, but not that of one able to wield much influence over others. He could not easily rid himself of the sarcastic expression continually playing round his mouth and flashing from his eyes, which gave him the air of a cold and impassible calculator; while nevertheless he was frequently ruled by his powerful imagination; sometimes led away by it to an extent befitting the most fantastic of visionaries.*[15]

Such was the man who rode alongside Cesare Borgia towards the betrayal which Cesare considered his 'beautiful deception'. By this time, lacking support of the powerful Venetians, which they had been counting upon, the revolt of the *condottieri* had run out of steam, and it was in attempting to re-pledge themselves to Cesare that they met their doom. He first led them to believe they were welcome back to the fold, but after they had served him in the capture of the Adriatic city of Sinigaglia, in December 1502, he sprang a trap as they rode in triumph through the city, and their four leaders were captured. Two were immediately strangled. The remaining pair, the brothers Francesco and Paulo Orsini, were very well-connected men, relatives of the powerful Cardinal Orsini. But Alexander freed Cesare of any concern by inviting the Cardinal to dinner in the Vatican, and poisoning him. The way cleared, Cesare had the Orsini brothers strangled.

Cesare's guile and ruthlessness could not fail to impress Machiavelli, who later wrote in *The Prince* that only 'inhuman cruelty' on the part of the commander could maintain unity and discipline in an army. As such, Cesare made an ideal executive, and his actions, to Machiavelli's mind, were exemplary. However, he did not maintain his high regard for Cesare, after the reign of the Borgias unravelled spectacularly. Rarely has a ruling house of such fearsome repute been laid low so quickly.

Cesare had long suffered venereal infection, the so-called 'French Disease'. Returning home in Rome in 1503, he got around the streets alone at night clad in black and masked to hide the syphilitic disfigurement of his once handsome features. On 12 August 1503, both Alexander and Cesare fell ill after a dinner in the Vatican, and Alexander died six days later. Talk abounded in Rome that they had both been accidentally stricken with poison intended for another dinner guest, but the most common view now is that they succumbed to a virulent fever rife that year. Alexander had been susceptible because of his years, and Cesare due to his advanced syphilis.

Though very seriously ill, Cesare sent his men in to ransack the Vatican treasury while he still had the chance, but it was the last stand of a desperate man. With Alexander dead, the French quickly cooled to Cesare, and while he was recovering the dispossessed rulers and cities of central Italy rallied against him. Cesare's troops—and with them his power—melted away into the countryside of the Romagna.

Confused perhaps by the sudden death of Alexander, the cardinals elected the elderly Pope Pius III, who himself died three weeks later. When the cardinals were again asked to decide on a pope, the old enemy of the Borgias, Cardinal Giuliano della Rovere, was the frontrunner. Enticed towards a deal to salvage some of his power, Cesare backed della Rovere, a surprise decision which Machiavelli later noted foundered on the foolish notion that unlike him, della Rovere would keep his word.

He didn't. Soon after his accession, Pope Julius II (his adopted name is suspected of being a pun at the expense of Cesare—'Caesar') had the former tyrant, now little more than a desperado on the run, arrested. Cesare was packed off home to Spain where life got little better for him, and he was cut down in a skirmish in 1507. He was 32. By then Machiavelli had turned from admiration to loathing, declaring 'He merited the most miserable of deaths.'

Cesare's sister Lucrezia, on the other hand, was seen to grow into the role of the Duchess of Ferrara, intelligent and capable. Though she possessed a massive and sumptuous wardrobe of gowns and hats, slippers and shoes, she was also considered generous to the poor and pious, praying in a hairshirt after the death of Cesare. She was administered the last rites of the Church before she died, aged just 39. As for her father Rodrigo, beyond his murders, schemes, affairs and bribes, he is remembered for some decorative changes to the Vatican, but mainly for the former.

✙ ✙ ✙

In October 2002 a major exhibition opened at the Palazzo Ruspoli in Rome, The Borgias: The Art of Power. It drew together more than two hundred artworks from museums around the world. In addition to Pinturicchio, who decorated the Borgia apartments in the Vatican, and who painted Giulia Farnese as the Virgin Mary for Alexander's bedchamber, other artists who met the Borgias, and whose works were part of the exhibition, included Michelangelo, Titian and Bellini. One room was dedicated solely to Cesare Borgia's military costumery.

Intent upon the question of whether the Borgias really were as bad as history has presented them, the exhibition's curators were keen to mount a strong defence. Co-curator and Borgia scholar Learco Andalo said at the opening, 'The aim of the show is to put the record straight. The Borgias are the victims of biased historical accounts based on malicious rumour.'[16]

While few could deny the ruthless machinations of Alexander and Cesare, the organisers in particular cast doubt upon the more scandalous stories, such as incest with Lucrezia. Co-curator Carlo Alfano said many allegations against Lucrezia were untrue, adding: 'Nor were claims that she had had an incestuous relationship with her father true, probably,'[17] and attested to the view that rumours of Borgia incest were spread by Lucrezia's jilted and disgruntled spouse, Giovanni Sforza.

Many historians concur that the accounts of incest were probably fabricated by Sforza, but that is not to say Alexander and Cesare did not behave in a scandalous manner in other respects, in particular the strong suspicion that Cesare raped Caterina Sforza. But it would appear with regard to Lucrezia at least, some basic human taboos were observed by the Borgias.

Some historians deem Lucrezia a woman wronged by previous generations whose stories became mingled with luridly colourful fictions about her, growing into a literary cottage industry which flourished during the nineteenth century. The Lucrezia industry shows little sign of slowing down. With new books, stage productions and films still being developed and released about her life, the name appears to retain its mystery and allure for authors, directors and public alike.

What then is the truth of the popular reputation of the Borgias as poisoners, which has rightly or wrongly persisted for centuries? It appears again that an intermingling of history and romantic fiction, and the fact that poisoning was rife during the Renaissance, may have led to this view.

The Borgias are said to have killed up to seventy of their rivals through poisoning, with some accounts having them killing people at a rate or one or two a week. In some versions Lucrezia's chef and poisoner worked side by side in her kitchens—surely very dangerous if they got their mixing bowls confused. Their poison of choice was popularly a white powder called *cantarella*, said to have had a pleasant taste but extremely toxic and leading quickly to death. Its purported use became the stuff of proverbs—which may have come from the Borgia's political foes—such as 'tasting the cup of the Borgias', a synonym for sudden, mysterious death.

According to the more macabre accounts, Alexander and Cesare experimented in applying arsenic to the entrails of freshly slaughtered beasts, from the decaying flesh of which they later harvested the fabled *cantarella*, less detectable and far more powerful than arsenic. Another version has the Borgias force-feeding arsenic to a bear, and extracting *cantarella* from its vomit.

Borgia biographer Marion Johnson, while pointing out that many people at the time were interested in trying to poison others, believes it was at best a very imprecise skill. 'Poisoning was an art practised all over Italy ... The science, however, was defective, and more was attempted than accomplished ... Legend portrays Cesare as an inveterate poisoner. No doubt he was interested, but the method was far too unsure for one who aimed to practise an efficient terror.'[18]

The curators of the The Borgias exhibition in 2002 refuted any inference that Lucrezia was a poisoner. 'Lucrezia poisoned no-one,' Learco Andalo stated. 'She was poisoned by the pen of history and nineteenth century Romanticism. She was instead a gifted stateswoman. She even ran the Vatican in her father's absence.'[19]

It would appear the jury is less decided, however, about whether Cesare was a poisoner. Nineteenth century historian Jacob Burckhardt considered that in addition to his fixer Don Michelotto, Cesare employed his own personal poisoner, a Spaniard called Sebastiano Pinzon.[20] Here too is Garrett Mattingly's assessment of Cesare. The bracketed words in the following quotation are Mattingly's own.

> It was said that he was his father's rival for his sister's bed. (Almost certainly false.) It was said that after the horrible sack of Capua he seized forty beautiful highborn maidens and added them to his personal harem. (Highly unlikely, Cesare does not seem to have shared his father's excessive appetite. The maidens were probably commandeered by Cesare's captains, though perhaps in his name.) It was said that he seduced that gallant youth Astorre Manfredi, and when he tired of him had him murdered. (Possibly, but the motive for the murder was more probably purely political.) It was said he murdered his brother, the Duke of Gandia. (Probable. At least his father seems to have believed it.) And that he had his brother-in-law, Lucrezia's second husband, murdered. (Pretty certainly true). But it was a dull week when one,

at least, of the embassies of Rome did not chalk up another murder
to Cesare's credit, sometimes by poison, sometimes by the hands of
hired assassins, sometimes by his own dagger. Probably he really was
responsible for a fair share of those bodies hauled out of the Tiber ...
As he marched through the anarchic Papal States, seizing one town
after another, by bribery or trickery or the sheer terror of his name, his
legend hung over him like a thundercloud.[21]

That thundercloud lifted with the deaths of Rodrigo and
Cesare Borgia. The final judgement on Rodrigo fell to the men
entrusted with his corpse, whose feelings may have mirrored those
of other ordinary Romans. '... the body was carried to the Chapel
of Santa Maria della Febbre and placed in its coffin next to the
wall in a corner by the altar. Six labourers or porters, making
blasphemous jokes about the pope and in contempt of his corpse,
together with two master carpenters, performed this task. The
carpenters had made the coffin too narrow and short, and so they
placed the pope's mitre at his side, rolled his body up in an old
carpet, and pummelled and pushed it into the coffin with their
fists. No wax tapers or lights were used, and no priests or other
persons attended to his body.'[22]

Other Borgias were to be active in religious and secular life
over the next two centuries,[23] but their reputations never reached the
same heights, or plumbed the same depths, as those of Rodrigo and
Cesare, and they never fired the popular imagination as Lucrezia
had done.

6. A NEW CAESAR

*... you can see various battles, and rapid actions
of figures, strange expressions on faces, costumes,
and an infinite number of things ...*

—LEONARDO DA VINCI, ON PAINTING

P ope Julius II was the warrior pontiff who truly did don
armour and lead his troops on horseback into battle.
By the same token, he was also a bold and visionary
patron of the arts, commissioning some of the finest art works of
the Renaissance. Whether or not he did take the name Julius as
a barb against his rival Cesare Borgia, Julius lived and acted as
much like a Roman general as a pope, a leader of men in battle
as well as shepherd to his flock of earthly sinners. Famed for his
battles with the Borgias and his arguments with his favourite artist
Michelangelo, Julius was literally larger than life.

He was born Giuliano della Rovere near Savona in 1443,
into a leading family fallen on hard times. He followed his uncle
Francesco della Rovere into the Franciscan Order. After Francesco
became Pope Sixtus IV in 1471, the elder della Rovere drew upon
his nephew's loyalty by charging him to lead a military campaign
against rebellions in the Papal States in 1474. The battlefield

experience Giuliano accrued would stand him in good stead in the many conflicts to come.

Sixtus IV made him a cardinal in 1479, in another pen stroke of papal nepotism. So widespread had this practice become that for generations a handful of Italian families dominated high church offices and papal elections. Four families accounted for ten popes in the two centuries from 1389 to 1605.[1]

After the death of Sixtus in 1484, Giuliano began a campaign of a different kind to have himself elected pope. He failed, and Innocent VIII ascended the throne. Eight years later Giuliano was again defeated, this time by the bribes of Rodrigo Borgia in 1492.

Giuliano denounced the Borgias to King Charles VIII of France, and accompanied him on the invasion of 1494, a military campaign which was to have far-reaching repercussions for the stability of the Italian peninsula. When the French ultimately returned home in tatters, having failed in their primary objective to overthrow Alexander, Giuliano went back with them, fearing for his life. He continued to plot against his archenemy from France.

He again contested the papal election following the death of Alexander VI in 1503, his way this time briefly blocked by the ailing Pius III, but at his fourth attempt Giuliano della Rovere gained the throne in October 1503.

Among his first acts was a decisive move against Cesare Borgia, the son of Alexander, whose military adventures had terrorised much of central Italy. Cesare fled to Spain where he died in battle in 1507.

Next Julius entered into a series of shifting alliances involving the French and other foreign powers, as well as the republic of Venice. After leading his army against a local despot in Perugia, he did what even Cesare had hesitated to do and moved against

Bologna, ruled by the despotic Bentivogli. The city surrendered to the Pope in November 1507 and he annexed it to the burgeoning Papal States.

Julius then turned his attention to the Venetians, who refused to give up the towns of Rimini and Faenza, which they themselves had taken from Cesare Borgia after his downfall. He joined forces with the Holy Roman Emperor Maximilian I and Louis XII of France in the League of Cambrai to face the Venetians, and inflicted a resounding defeat on them in May 1509. Venice was forced to terms, and the disputed cities restored to the Pope.

But having achieved his goal against Venice, Julius next solicited their support against his erstwhile allies the French, exhorting the Venetians to help him drive the foreigners out of Italy. To this end he formed the Holy League in 1511, in alliance with Venice, Spain, England, and Emperor Maximilian. The French were decisively defeated at Ravenna the following year, and for the second time in less than two decades sent packing over the Alps back into France. By this time, through his mastery of the art of diplomacy and his strategic skills as a general, Julius had expanded the borders of the Papal States far beyond the dreams of the Borgias, who had tried so long and hard for the same end.

Despite all this, the Pope managed to work in his spiritual duties, saying Mass daily and exerting himself against some corrupt practices, such as papal electoral bribery and simony. He also found time to lay the foundation stone for the new Saint Peter's Basilica, designed by Donato Bramante, and was the renowned patron of artists such as Michelangelo and Raphael.

The gargantuan basilica—its awe-inspiring dimensions attesting in brick and mortar to the scale of the man Julius considered himself to be—replaced the thousand year old church over the grave of Saint Peter, and was mired in controversy from the outset. Bramante's rivals fulminated against the Pope and against the design, saying the cost would be ruinous and would demand ever higher taxation, and construction would be inevitably drawn out. By the time the biggest church in Christendom was completed more than a century later, in 1626, much of the original plan had been slashed or changed, but the edifice which Julius ordered built has stood at the centre of the Christian world ever since, an abiding symbol of Catholic prestige and power.[2]

Although Michelangelo is famed for his commissions from Julius, most notably the ceiling of the Sistine Chapel, he and the Pope had a notoriously fractious and sometimes fiery relationship. Matters plumbed their depths when Julius offered and Michelangelo grasped what many might consider the ultimate poisoned chalice, the commission to build the finest, and certainly the most grandiose, tomb in all of Christendom.

Relations between patron and artist over plans and budget soured to such a point that when Michelangelo visited Rome in early 1506, the Pope refused to see him. Faced with a patron as wilful and passionate as himself, the young artist put Rome and the project behind him, fuming in a letter he sent to papal architect Giuliano da Sangallo.

> *I learn from a letter sent by you that the Pope was angry at my departure, that he is willing to place the money at my disposal and to carry out what was agreed upon between us; also that I am to come back and fear nothing. As far as my departure is concerned, the truth is that on Holy Saturday I heard the Pope, speaking at table with a jeweller and the Master of Ceremonies, say he did not want to spend another baiocco on stones whether small or large, which surprised me very much. However, before I set out, I asked him for some of the money required for continuance of my work. His Holiness replied that*

I was to come back again on Monday, and I went on Monday, and on Tuesday, and on Wednesday, and on Thursday, as His Holiness saw. At last, on the Friday morning, I was turned out, that is to say, I was driven away; and the person who turned me away said he knew who I was, but that such were his orders. Thereupon, having heard those words on Saturday and seeing them afterwards put into execution, I lost all hope. But this alone was not the whole reason for my departure. There was also another cause but I do not wish to write about it; enough that it made me think that, if I were to remain in Rome, my own tomb would be prepared before that of the Pope.[3]

The episode was to have a sequel. Several months later Michelangelo was summoned back to Rome to face the Pope, who asked him why he had left the city. 'Michelangelo answered, "Not from ill will, but from disdain (*ma per disdegno*)." ' A bishop who was present nervously intervened, 'Pay no attention, your Holiness; he speaks out of ignorance. Artists are all like that.'[4] At that the artistic temper exploded and blows were exchanged before Michelangelo was ejected from the papal chamber.

After that falling out, the imperious Julius would leave the impetuous Michelangelo in no doubt about who ruled. To celebrate his conquest of Bologna, the Pope commissioned a large bronze statue for the church of San Patronio. It took Michelangelo a year to finish, and upon its completion the Pope had it smashed to pieces and melted down. Following that humiliation, Michelangelo returned to his native Florence, swearing to have nothing more to do with Rome. But Julius had other ideas—indeed, a very big idea, the Sistine Chapel. The ceiling had already been painted, by Pier Matteo Serdenti d'Amelia, but Julius considered it lacklustre and mediocre, and so in 1508 Michelangelo again found himself under commission to the Vicar of Rome.

The work provided unique challenges in subject matter, perspective, in angles and planes, and in pure stamina on the part of the artist—although we are unsure that he painted, as legend has it, for four years lying on the flat of his back. It has also been said that Michelangelo might well have regarded the Chapel ceiling as another poisoned chalice, as sculpture and not painting was his preferred form. As such it required him to go far beyond anything he had done before and, unusually for the times, he was left to work out the subject matter for himself. But he was the right artist for the almost superhuman task. Whatever faults Julius might have had, he knew the artist of his age, and ensured it was the irascible Florentine who painted his ceiling.

Michelangelo chose as his subject the Biblical epic of Creation, the Downfall of Humanity, and the yearning promise of Salvation. The end result astonished viewers, as it still does today; and visitors still queue to enter the chapel. The very first viewing, though, was the most climactic.

'When, on 31 October 1512 the frescoes were officially unveiled, artists and connoisseurs were prepared for something which should change the course of painting; and that, in fact, is what it did; and not only painting, but the whole mode of feeling. The freshness and wonder of the early Renaissance, the delight in living things unburdened with a conscience, birds, children, flowers—all this was crushed by the oppressive awareness of human destiny.'[5]

✠　✠　✠

Scholars have long praised the contribution Julius made to the cultural heritage of humanity through patronage of Michelangelo and Raphael. British Renaissance scholar John R. Hale described Pope Julius II as 'one of the most intelligent and forceful art patrons the world has ever known', adding that he set artists 'fierce challenges'.

'By 1509, aged 26, Raphael had arrived in Rome and was working for Julius. First he did the frescoes in the room called the Stanza della Signatura or Signature Room in the Vatican. The theme, or program, for the frescoes was probably drawn up by the Pope for his humanist advisers, and was extremely complicated. But Raphael succeeded in producing a cycle of paintings which has variously been called the pictorial encyclopaedia of humanism and the apotheosis of the classical style.'[6]

Kenneth Clark also lauded the wisdom with which Julius handled his commissions. 'The most profound thought of the time was not expressed in words, but in visual imagery. Two sublime examples of this truism were produced in the same building in Rome, not more than one hundred yards from each other and during exactly the same years: Michelangelo's ceiling of the Sistine Chapel and Raphael's frescoes in the Stanza della Signatura. Both of them we owe entirely to Julius II.

Over centuries writers on Michelangelo have criticised Julius for taking him off the tomb commission, on which he had set his heart, and putting him to work on the painting of the Sistine Ceiling, although he had always said he hated the act of painting, but it was a stroke of inspiration. The original project for the tomb included almost forty marble figures, larger than life-size. How could Michelangelo ever have completed it? We know that he carved marble faster than any mason, but even with his heroic energy the tomb would have taken twenty years, during which time his mind was changing and developing. And the very fact that, on the ceiling, he decided to illustrate themes, not merely to concentrate on single figures, freed him to extend his thoughts about human relationships and human destiny.[7]

In his sixties Pope Julius's health began to fail, and he died, very peacefully for a man who had once led troops into the heat of battle, in February 1513. He bequeathed to Rome enlarged territories and a very healthy treasury, and to humanity a treasury of art, a legacy which today still provokes admiration, awe and argument.[8]

7. THE MEDICI AND THE TIARA: LEONINE PRIDE

'To wear about his neck, he had a golden chain, weighing twenty-five thousand and sixty-three marks of gold, the links thereof made after the manner of great berries, amongst which were set in work green jaspers, and cut dragon-like, all environed with beams and sparks ...'

—RABELAIS, *GARGANTUA*

The banking dynasty Giovanni de' Medici founded in the closing decade of the fourteenth century would flourish for four hundred years, up to the death of the 'last of the Medici', Anna Maria Ludovica, in 1743.[1] Among the luminaries were two popes and two cardinals, a king, Louis XIII of France, and four queens. These included Henrietta Maria of France, the Medici who married England's Charles I.[2]

The two popes were Leo X and Clement VII, the sons of Lorenzo the Magnificent and his brother Giuliano. Giuliano had fallen to an assassin's blade in the Pazzi conspiracy of Easter 1478, and Lorenzo raised Giuliano's illegitimate infant son Giulio (born only weeks before his father's murder) with his own sons, including Giovanni, a boy three years Giulio's senior.

The rise of Giovanni de' Medici (1475–1521) towards the papal office was nothing if not meteoric. He was only 13 when made a cardinal (although not permitted to take up the post until 17), and was elected pope at the age of only 37, one of the youngest ever to wear the tiara. Although among the favoured candidates, he was far from a certainty. His relative youth, which threatened a long period in office and could thus prevent other older cardinals from ever holding the post, was against him, and the votes were only tied up after a group of cardinals had been reassured that his health was poor and he would not live long as pope.[3]

Having swayed the Conclave, he took the name Leo X, one long associated with distinction among popes.[4] His papacy, and that of his cousin Giulio as Clement VII, was shared with two other young and determined men who defined the era in Europe, the impetuous Francois I of France, and the more reserved Holy Roman Emperor Charles V. Through historical twists of fate, it was the troops of Charles V, and not the menacing imperial forces of the Sultan of Turkey, who would ultimately sack Rome. In many respects, all four of these men embodied to some extent or other what came to be referred to as that creature of the High Renaissance, the 'Renaissance Man'.[5]

Lorenzo the Magnificent described his three sons respectively as foolish, shrewd and good. Giovanni, the middle son, was the shrewd. It was just as well he was intelligent as there was little other obvious magnificence about him, and few would have picked him as a Renaissance Man: the physical presence alone of the young pope gave little encouragement to those who might have cherished hopes for his pontificate.

'Like his father before him, Leo was physically unprepossessing. His head was huge, almost deformed in its size, and his body too was so massive that seated he gave the appearance of a very large man. Standing he lost something of his majesty for his legs were ludicrously short and spindly so that he seemed to scuttle rather than walk. His protuberant eyes, set in a fat red face, were painfully shortsighted.'[6] The news for his new subjects was not all bad though. 'But in contrast to his ungainly body was his attractive personality. He spoke clearly and lucidly in a soft, rather gentle voice and laughed often and spontaneously. He was genuinely interested in people, caring nothing for their social standing, demanding only that they should amuse him.'[7]

Accounts agree that Leo was an urbane man, easygoing, with tastes extending to clowning, buffoonery and *burlesco*, even to what could now be called carnival and freak shows.

> *In Pope Leo X, the genuine Florentine love of jesters showed itself strikingly. The prince, whose taste for the most refined intellectual pleasures was insatiable, endured and desired at his table a number of witty buffoons and merry-andrews, among them two monks and a cripple; at public feasts he treated them with deliberate scorn as parasites, setting before them monkeys and crows in the place of savoury meats. Indeed, Leo showed a peculiar fondness for the burla; it was characteristic of his nature sometimes to treat his favourite pursuits—music and poetry—ironically, parodying them with his factotum, Cardinal Bibbiena. Neither of them found it beneath his dignity to fool an honest old secretary till he thought himself a master of the art of music. The Improvisatore, Baraballo of Geta, was brought so far by Leo's flattery that he applied in all seriousness for the poet's coronation on the Capitol. On the feast day of Saints Cosmas and Damian, the patrons of the house of Medici, he was first compelled, adorned with laurel and purple, to amuse the papal guests with his recitations, and at last, when all were ready to split with laughter, to mount a gold-harnessed elephant in the court of the Vatican, sent as a*

present to Rome by Emmanuel the Great of Portugal, while the Pope looked down from above through his eyeglass. But the animal was so terrified by the noise of the trumpets and kettledrums and cheers of the crowd, there was no getting him over the bridge of Sant'Angelo.[8]

In addition to a love of jests, practical jokes and witty repartee, Leo had a penchant for table games, including chess, and other interests which marked him apart from many of his predecessors. He had a love of hunting too, and would set off with full entourage of well over a hundred on fishing trips and hunts for wild boar, deer and game birds.

Above and beyond these favoured pursuits, however, he was most famous for another pastime which might render him a figure some modern readers may relate to more readily: he loved spending money. That is why, in addition to his fostering of arts and culture (almost de rigueur in Renaissance Italy anyway) his time in the Vatican is sometimes referred to as the 'Golden Age'. It was certainly a time when the Pope's men literally flung gold coins by the fistful into the streets as a crowd-pleaser. The ability to toss money about was in part a by-product of being the heir to one of Europe's richest banking dynasties, but also from the very well-stacked coffers left by Julius II, a treasury of almost a million ducats. Leo also had personal income—not directly derived from the papal office, as the pope is unpaid—of several hundred thousand ducats a year, a huge sum for the era. The money was there to be spent, and Leo was just the pope to spend it.

The cost of being a Renaissance Man was high: monuments, artists, scholars, even poets didn't come cheap. And in terms of patronage, the popes sat at the apex of the cultural big spenders of the late Middle Ages. The papal curia expected him to spend money, the nobility expected it, and so did the people. As for the great flock of illiterate and semi-literate faithful off in the wilder realms of Christendom, they expected nothing less of the ruler of glorious fabled Rome.

> The greatest of the fifteenth-century Italian patrons in terms of money was the papacy ... Sixtus IV (1471–1484) who began the alterations at St Peter's, built the famous chapel that bears his name (the 'Sistine'), employed Botticelli, Ghirlandaio, Perugino, Signorelli and other noted artists, and chose as his librarian the papal biographer Platina. His successors, Innocent VIII and Alexander VI, gave work to Mantegna and Pinturicchio, but the greatest products of papal patronage, the building of a new St Peter's, the addition of many suites of rooms to the Vatican palace, and the re-planning of much of Rome, were to be the work of the sixteenth century. To emphasise their rank, which placed them above the merely temporal rulers of Italy, the popes determined to outshine all others as patrons. Their activities came to a peak when princely and pontifical pride joined together in the Medici popes Leo X and Clement VII.[9]

Indeed, so determined was Leo to glitter that he spent Medici money as well as the papal treasury on urban beautification and the construction of palaces, and on acquiring art and other fine objects. He spent it enticing scholars to his papal court (although he did not invite two of the sharpest quills of the times, Erasmus and Machiavelli). The attractions of Humanism were all too plain to Leo and he was even quoted as remarking: 'How very profitable this fable of Christ has been to us through the ages.'[10] With a pope fond of a joke, the comment may have been a little less than serious, but it remains indicative of the kind of man installed in Rome. He also inevitably spent vast sums on political connections and others he wished to foster, on friends, and even, it appears, on his subjects.

Renowned Reformation historian G.R. Elton[11] styled Leo as 'soft and kindly'[12], and as such he was not so temperamentally disposed to patronage of the favoured artist of his predecessor Julius, the headstrong and irascible Michelangelo Buonarroti. Instead, he preferred to call upon the services of the up and coming Raffaello (Raphael) Sanzio.

Raphael was born in Urbino in 1483, into the family of an artist father who gave him his first tuition in painting. Urbino had prospered under the enlightened rule of Duke Federico da Montefeltro, and the child Raphael breathed the gentle air of a cultured capital. He studied with Perugino in Perugia, and by his late teens was already considered a master. Excited by reports of the impact being made in Florence by the works of Michelangelo and Leonardo da Vinci,[13] he moved there and began to understudy them.

Still in his mid twenties, Raphael painted a series of Madonnas, as well as several of his best-known works, including his *Annunciation*, *Adoration of the Magi* and *Crucifixion* (all 1502–03). He also became well acquainted with the power and influence of the Medici, a connection which would open new horizons for him.

It was at the suggestion of Bramante, architect of the new Saint Peter's, that Julius II summoned the young Raphael to Rome in 1508. There he spent the last twelve years of his short life working at a frantic pace, creating what we have come to regard as some of the finest masterpieces of Western art.

While Michelangelo laboured nearby on the Sistine Chapel ceiling, Julius put Raphael to work decorating Le Stanze, the papal apartments, with majestic paintings celebrating the history of the Church. While the *Dispute* is considered a pièce de résistance of Roman Church triumphalism, the other most famous work from Le Stanze, the *School of Athens*, celebrates an unbroken thread of human philosophical inquiry stretching back to Plato and Aristotle, and is considered a masterpiece of Humanism.

After the accession of Leo X to the throne, a complex of new tasks lay ahead for Raphael. At the time there was a growing awareness of the heritage of ancient Rome, from the ruins of which the Renaissance city was springing. Scholar Poggio Bracciolini decried the state into which ancient Rome had been allowed to fall, saying it 'now lies prostrate like a giant corpse, decayed and everywhere eaten away'.[14]

Besides the inevitable sun, wind and rain, another powerful element was eating away at the ruins of old Rome: fashion. All kinds of objects being pillaged from the ruins—statues, monuments, pillars, and household items—were invested with the cachet of chic by wealthy collectors during the economic boom time of Julius II and Leo X. Workers unearthed pieces including famed sculptures such as the *Apollo Belvedere* and the *Vatican Venus*. To his considerable credit, Leo moved to protect the city's heritage by appointing Raphael as superintendent of Roman antiquities, to survey and protect what remained, especially charging him to preserve original inscriptions 'for the promotion of literature and the cultivation of the Latin tongue'.[15]

One could only hope that Rome's antiquities were better cared for by their superintendent than was the Pantheon. Commissioned to make a grand altar sculpture for the new St Peter's, but strapped for cash and materials, Raphael stripped the bronze ceiling from the Pantheon, considered one of the loveliest buildings of antiquity, and melted it down. In a twist of fate, the Pantheon would later become the artist's final resting place.

It was the death of Bramante, however, which gave Raphael his greatest challenge. 'I have taken over the construction of Saint Peter's from Bramante,' he wrote. 'What city in the world is greater than Rome and what building greater than St Peter's? It is the chief temple of the world—the largest building that has ever been seen. It is going to cost over a million in gold and I can assure you that the Pope is determined to spend 60,000 ducats on it during the coming year, and can think of nothing else.'[16]

In addition to the staggering cost of the building, big enough even to rob a Medici banker of sleep, there had been the ongoing open hostility between Bramante and the man who would ultimately complete his grand plan, his rival Michelangelo. The men were entirely different in character, Michelangelo driven and ascetic in habits, Bramante highfalutin and inclining to the sybaritic. So deeply did their rivalry and mutual dislike run that it was Bramante who suggested to Pope Julius that Michelangelo should paint the Sistine Ceiling, considering the task beyond the scope of Michelangelo's best abilities, and beyond the powers of any one artist.

When it came to Saint Peter's, the feuding between the two men became even more heated. Once his plans were approved, Bramante was impatient to get on with the job, pressing ahead with the demolition of the old St Peter's, which had served since the fourth century as the heart of Christendom, and beneath which the bones of Saint Peter themselves were interred. Bramante started clearing the site with such gusto that he acquired the nickname 'The Demolisher'. Michelangelo quarrelled with him about what he saw as wanton destruction of elements of the old structure, such as its massive pillars, assembled from pagan temples of ancient Rome by Constantine after his conversion. Bramante was in no mood whatever to respect any heritage listing suggested by his rival, and pressed on.

Michelangelo would have the last laugh, however. Perhaps because of his abstemious habits, he outlived Bramante by decades, (and also outlived Raphael). In 1546, more than thirty years after the death of his rival and four decades after Julius had given his imprimatur to Bramante's design, the now septuagenarian Michelangelo was chosen by Pope Paul III to re-design and complete Saint Peter's Basilica.

To contemporary eyes the original design is quite tawdry, more like a Victorian bus terminus. Over the decades it was re-worked towards the design for what would become one of the most widely recognised buildings on earth, and from Michelangelo's hand it gained its most distinguishing feature, 'crowning it with the grandiose cupola which was to be forever connected with his name and with the monumental profile of the Eternal City.'[17]

✥   ✥   ✥

Inevitably the Age of Leo could not be golden for all. Although he showered patronage far and wide, some would miss out and resentment fester. Disenfranchised elements found a focus in the affair of the young Lorenzo, grandson of Lorenzo the Magnificent.

After the death of Julius II, only one relative of significance, his nephew Francesco Maria della Rovere, remained in a position of real power. As Duke of Urbino, Francesco held sway over one of the richest and most culturally desirable city-states of Italy. The hostility between the Medici and the della Rovere families went back generations, and it was no great feat for Leo to conjure up reasons why Julius's nephew Francesco should be removed from Urbino. With the aid of French troops the city fell, and Leo's own nephew, Lorenzo, was installed as duke. But Francesco refused to go quietly, and a lengthy and expensive war ensued, depleting the coffers of a pope already financially overcommitted. Worse for Leo, near fatal in fact, was the agitation of the usurped Francesco within the college of cardinals, which precipitated one of the most insidious plots in the history of the papacy.

The originator of the so-called Conspiracy of the Cardinals was Cardinal Alfonso Petrucci, a young man who harboured a deep-seated family resentment against the Medici. In early 1517 he met little trouble gathering others to his cause, including cardinals with close connections to the ousted Francesco della Rovere. The plan was simple: to stage a coup d'etat by poisoning the pope. The opportunity was afforded by the lavish living which endeared the pope to many of his followers. Rome was famed for its dinner parties, with bizarre and extravagant dishes, such as the tongues of parrots, served up on solid gold plates. Like many gourmands and bon vivants, Leo suffered a problem of the digestive tract, in this case an ulcer at the very terminus of that tract, which presented an opening for murder.

'Leo was still being treated for a dangerous and painful anal ulcer. During the timely indisposition of the pope's own physician, Petrucci planned to introduce a physician of his own choice who would mingle poison with the ointment intended for the treatment of the ulcer. The plan would have succeeded had not Leo, with a fortunate delicacy, declined to be treated by a stranger.'[18]

The affair might have ended there, but word seeped out, through Petrucci's own carelessness, and he was arrested and incarcerated in the Vatican's keep, the forbidding tower of Castel Sant'Angelo. The application of searing irons to the flesh of the young cardinal soon delivered up the names of a cabal of conspirators, including a personal friend of Leo's, Adrian of Corneto, and Cardinal Riario, a senior cardinal who had run close to Leo in the Conclave that had elected him. During the

investigation it was revealed that sympathies among the cardinals
ran strongly counter to Leo, and he was left to demand despairingly,
'what more could I have given you all?'

After another bout of torture, Petrucci was hanged. Riario
and the other conspirators either managed to extract papal
mercy, or fled into exile. Still puzzled by the revolt of so many
for whom he felt he had done so much, Leo ensured it did not
happen again through the creation of some thirty new cardinals,
more than enough allies in the consistory to guarantee his sway.
At the same time, the fees paid for each cardinal's hat eased his
tightening fiscals. To many observers, it was a very Medici ending
to the affair.

✛ ✛ ✛

Money remained very tight though. Besides all the other demands
upon the papal purse, the ongoing construction of Saint Peter's was
a financial haemorrhage, and to maintain cash flow to the builders
Leo became ever more deeply involved in the business of indulgences,
a trade which would soon cost the Church extremely dearly.

Four years after Leo's election as pope, in a city far to the
north of Italy, an event took place which would change the course
of history not just of the Church, but of nations, for centuries.
Although there had been disquiet about corrupt practices within
the Church for generations, it was the sale of indulgences which
brought matters to a head, prompting Martin Luther to nail his
theses to the door of the palace church in the German city of
Wittenberg on 31 October 1517.[19]

Put simply, a papal indulgence was the mediaeval equivalent
of the 'Get Out Of Jail Free' card of the Monopoly board game. An

indulgence could be purchased from God's representative on earth, the Pope, to reduce the amount of time a sinner had to spend in painful penance in Purgatory after their death, before their final promotion up to Heaven.[20] As all men and women were sinners, a vast amount of Purgatory 'debt' was accrued throughout Christendom, meaning the sale of Purgatory 'credits' tapped a literally unlimited market.

The issue of the sale of indulgences had long been a cause of debate among Church scholars, clergy and congregation. Erasmus had acidly pilloried it before Luther, in 1509, in his book *In Praise of Folly*, in which he lumps the purveyors of indulgences with those who peddle superstitions to the weak and gullible, those who pray before images and shrines to saints, and those who pray before Saint George, whom Erasmus likens to the 'Hercules of the pagans'. But he saves his most withering cadences for indulgences:

'What shall I say of such as cry up and maintain the cheat of indulgences? That by these compute the time of each soul's residence in purgatory, and assign them a longer or shorter continuance, according as they purchase more or fewer of these paltry pardons, and saleable exemptions?' Such practices he portrays as about as useful as prayer before an image of himself: 'Or if any pray to Erasmus on such particular holidays, with the ceremony of wax candles and other fopperies, he shall in a short time be rewarded with a plentiful increase of wealth and riches.'[21]

Despite the objections of Christian thinkers and scholars like Erasmus, the practice had grown over time, beginning when popes issued indulgences in special circumstances, such as the Crusades. By the late Middle Ages it had flourished into something approximating a mediaeval futures market.

'Though official doctrine was always careful to stress the need for genuine penitence and the impossibility of obtaining valid remission of sins by merely buying an indulgence, the manner in which the business was represented to the people was much cruder. In practise it came to be thought that by the act of buying a papal indulgence men could at least shorten their own time in Purgatory, and by the fifteenth century it was commonly held that the souls of the dead in Purgatory could also be helped by indulgences bought on their behalf. Though indulgences were always proclaimed for an ostensibly religious purpose—a crusade, or the building of a cathedral—they came in fact to be no more than an important source of papal revenue.'[22]

While no-one could escape a term in Purgatory entirely, through the judicious purchase of an indulgence, a Christian could wipe a large span of years from the time he would otherwise expect to spend suffering there for pardoned sins. Such pardoned sins were differentiated from unpardoned mortal sins, for which the sinner was dispatched to Hell, an irredeemable plight. It was also a place where those who had committed venial, or more minor sins, were sent, awaiting promotion up to Heaven.

Although the matter of indulgences had long been debated, it crystallised in the consecration of the young new archbishop of Mainz in Germany, Albert of Hohenzollern. He was required to pay more than 20,000 ducats to Rome for his promotion, and had borrowed the money from Europe's richest bank, the Fuggers, and now the Fuggers wanted their repayments. Leo did a deal to assist the young archbishop through the sale of papal indulgences to the faithful flock, with proceeds to be split fifty-fifty between Leo and Albert (and hence the Fuggers), in the case of Leo to help pay for the war against the Turks, the fabulous expense of building Saint Peter's, and numerous sundry outgoings.

'The sale was very efficiently advertised; despite perfunctory safeguards, the stress lay on the chance offered to people to buy themselves and their relatives out of so much time in the fires of purgatory by a money payment which would enable them to participate in the merits of the saints without going through the tiresome business of contrition, absolution and penance. Moreover, the business was put in the hands of crude salesmen like the Dominican John Tertzel who operated near Wittenberg.'[23]

Tertzel's sales pitch was to the point, like a modern day hawker flogging steak-knives or thermal underwear on late night television, a kind of one-man ecclesiastical shopping channel. 'I have here the passports ... to lead the human soul into Paradise. Inasmuch as for a single one of the mortal sins, several of which are committed every day after confession, seven years of expiation either on earth or in Purgatory are imposed—who for the sake of a quarter florin would hesitate to secure one of these letters which will admit your divine, immortal soul to the celestial joys of paradise?'[24]

Business boomed and cash poured in, but the huckstering of Tertzel and his ilk raised hackles, and none was more hackled than the monk Martin Luther. He had visited Rome and stood horrified before the decadent excess of the Vatican elite. Now he saw Rome financing its extravagances through an outrageous sales pitch to the uneducated poor and needy.

Even though such practices were forbidden in his own diocese, Luther's congregation flocked in boats across the Elbe to Tertzel and his men, florins in hands outstretched. 'Luther's souls were crossing the river and bringing back bits of paper to prove their freedom from sin. They found their pastor mountingly indignant and distressed.'[25]

It was only a matter of time until Luther was at the church door, hammer in hand, nailing up his 95 theses. While centrally concerned with the entire tawdry business of indulgences, Luther

appeared to recognise the stimulus for the latest sales drive originating courtesy of the pope's monumental construction of St Peter's, noting specifically in thesis 86:

'Again, why does not the pope, whose wealth is today greater than the wealth of the richest Crassus, build this one basilica of Saint Peter with his own money rather than with the money of poor believers?'[26]

Luther appears to have asked his questions in the best of faith, as a means of opening up real debate within the Church about its direction and practices, but with other clergy immediately at odds with the dissident German, Leo felt comfortable to consign the entire matter to a 'monkish squabble'. After all, the Church had dealt successfully enough with this kind of thing before, riding out reformers like the Englishman John Wycliffe and the Bohemian Jan Hus back in the fourteenth century. Viewing Luther as little more than a heretic, Leo excommunicated him, but did not trouble himself with many further measures. The monk's effigy was burned in public and he was forced to retreat to a mountain hideaway, and Leo felt reassured the danger had passed, even when warning signs reappeared as Luther started to garner followers across Germany.

The year 1517 had been a busy one, but having seen off the conspiratorial cardinals, and judging there was little to fear in the German monk, Leo would have felt pleased at last to return to the contemplation of his fine objets d'art and dining on parrots' tongues, all crises passed. It was not to be.

✛   ✛   ✛

Political problems were gathering, and they would especially vex Leo's cousin Giulio who would follow him as Clement VII. The chickens let loose by Julius II, when he urged French king Charles VIII to invade Italy and depose the Borgia pope Alexander VI, were about to come home to roost. France's campaign of 1494 and subsequent French military involvement in various theatres of hostility in Italy helped bring about an instability in the Italian peninsula that would last for many decades yet.

In 1513, the year that Julius died, the French had marched back into Italy to assert Louis XII's claims to Milan and Naples. Early in his pontificate Leo had been forced into an alliance with the Spanish against France. The French were defeated and left, but as soon as their new king Francois ascended the throne in 1515, they were at it again. Leo had once again been forced into an alliance with Spain and England, but on this occasion it was Francois who triumphed, and Leo forced to terms. It reached crisis point again in 1519 when the underlying tensions came into sharp focus through the rivalry between Francois and the Habsburg heir Charles I, who defeated him in the election for the post of Holy Roman Emperor, and became Emperor Charles V.

The son of ('Mad') Juana, the daughter of Isabella and Ferdinand of Spain, and Philip of Castile, Charles was born in Ghent (now in Belgium) in 1500. Through an almost historically uniquely opportune series of inheritances, before he left his teens he had become ruler of Castile, Burgundy, Luxembourg, the Netherlands, Aragon, Sicily, Naples, and the ever increasing and profitable Spanish possessions in the Americas, the New World to which his grandparents had financed Columbus. As such, the ruler of Spain was one of the most powerful people in the known world, if not the most. Yet another inheritance ensured he asserted that power.

'In January 1519, his other grandfather, the Emperor Maximilian, also died, leaving Charles heir to the Austrian lands (Austria, Tyrol, Styria, Carintha, Carniola) and the original Habsburg family lands round the Upper Rhine, between Switzerland and Burgundy. (Maximilian's death) also vacated the crown of the Holy Roman Empire.'[27]

The young man who inherited such enormous power and wealth was, like Leo X, rather unprepossessing at first sight, being, according to accounts from the time, '... a slight, rather ugly man with a reserved manner. His mind was slow, but though unoriginal, far from negligible. He suffered from a high sense of duty and a powerful conviction of God's demands upon him.'[28]

He was nonetheless devout, a patron of the arts (though in a more understated and less ostentatious manner than some of his contemporaries), and showed skill, perspicacity, some panache, and above all perseverance in holding together an empire which stretched from the lowlands of Holland to the peaks of Tyrolea, from the Bay of Naples to the hub of Castille, Madrid, the capital he would dub 'Crowned and Imperial'.While at one point it seemed that yet another young monarch, England's Henry VIII would toss his hat into the ring for Holy Roman Emperor, in the end the only serious challenge to Charles came from Francois I, with whom he would share an almost lifelong rivalry.

Variously described as intelligent, passionate and impetuous, lecherous and tyrannical, the young Frenchman had imperial ambitions and visions of military glory, as well as a love of arts and culture, and the personal charm of a Renaissance Man. He revelled in the outdoors and the hunt, boasting 'when he was old he could have himself carried after the hounds, that when he was dead he would hunt in his coffin',[29] yet he also wrote poetry and was a lover of books, which he collected with zeal. He encouraged French exploration in the Americas to counter Spanish dominance, was a patron of the controversial author Rabelais, and laid the foundations for the Louvre. Francois was the owner of a painting by Leonardo da Vinci which would become a global art icon, *Mona Lisa*,[30] and invited the artist to live in France.

Francois was also a patron of Erasmus. The Dutch thinker and writer Desiderius Erasmus entered and departed an Augustinian monastery as a young man, lived in England where he taught Greek at Cambridge, and was a friend of the writer and philosopher Thomas More. While still counted among the faithful, and certainly no Protestant, Erasmus gained renown for his barbed criticism of hypocrisy and corruption in the Church, as well as for his moderating approval of the new Humanist values spreading through Europe. It is not surprising that Francois, a king who spent much of his life in campaigns against popes and the Holy Roman Emperor would find interest in the works of such a man as Erasmus.

But the dashing young Francois lacked something which the less than dashing Charles possessed in troves: money. Charles's vast territories yielded healthy finances, as did the astronomical riches of the German banking family the Fuggers, which had allowed him unmatchable spending when it came to bribing the seven electors throughout the Holy Roman Empire to vote him the crown. 'It was the Fuggers who paid for all this ... they were ardent Catholics, fierce and damaging opponents of Luther and the Reformation ... they and they alone made it possible for Charles to carry on his tense struggle for the Imperial crown in the teeth of the fantastic bribes of the French king. Without the Fuggers, it is almost certainly true to say, the Habsburgs could never have emerged from the Middle Ages as a major power. The activities of this remarkable family carried them into every corner of European commerce and finance. Their imagination, allied with shrewdness, was unlimited. Their wealth was past computing. They were the kingmakers.'[31]

Francois was defeated, the election of Charles was unanimous, and in June 1519, still eight months shy of his twentieth birthday, this pale young man ascended the most powerful secular throne in Christendom, and became its Emperor.

Francois was galled by the loss to Charles: the pair faced off across the Pyrenees, and both courted Leo as an ally in the struggle they knew was coming. Loath to take sides, and despite promises to the contrary, Leo ultimately joined with Charles, uniting Papal with Imperial troops. Like his predecessor Julius, he began a campaign to drive the French northwards out of the peninsula. Their combined forces had just won a decisive victory at Parma in northern Italy when Leo, who had been unwell for a week or so, died on 1 December 1521. Although poisoning was suspected, nothing was ever proved, and it appears he died happy at the news from the battlefield, and in the belief his earthly domain had been secured.

✛ ✛ ✛

The realm which Leo left was in no respect as secure as it might have appeared. He had emptied the Vatican treasury, leaving Rome near bankruptcy. Moreover, power had shifted from the Church to the bankers, who had grown fat on ecclesiastical booty from debts such as that owed by the young Archbishop of Mainz. The bankers also profited from the rising artisan class across Europe, at that time beginning the long process of sloughing off the mediaeval yoke of kings and nobles. Perhaps one should not be so surprised that this deep shift went on during the 'Golden Age' of Leo, the first pontificate of the banking dynasty, the Medici.

8. THE MEDICI AND THE TIARA: INCLEMENT TIMES

The world is all a carcass and vanity,
The shadow of a shadow, a play

—MONTAIGNE

In 1523, two years after the death of Leo, another Medici would ascend the papal throne. But first there was the brief interregnum of the Dutchman, Adrian of Utrecht. Adrian had been tutor to Charles V during the emperor's tender years, and the grown-up Charles now used his sizeable leverage in the Conclave of Cardinals to have his old mentor elected pope.

Adrian knew little of the ways of Rome, was found to be rather less than a Renaissance Man, and early in his papacy was judged entirely unsuitable by a number of his peers, '... a barbarian who had been horrified at the pagan splendours of the Vatican when he at length arrived there. Barely able to speak Latin, Adrian seemed to believe that the prime duty of the supreme pontiff was to give spiritual guidance and set a Christian example to Christians.'[1]

This would not do, not for the bon vivants of Rome. Like Leo
before him, Adrian too misread the growing crisis in Germany
with the followers of Luther, and suffered setbacks in the ongoing
struggle with the Turks, the most serious being the loss of the
strategic island of Rhodes in 1522. But more than anything else,
it was Adrian's style which rankled with the Roman elite, and
following his timely death in 1523, many among the ruling clans
of Rome looked forward to a resumption of business as usual.
After all, another Medici candidate was before the cardinals in the
person of Giulio de' Medici, cousin of Leo X, son of Giuliano, and
nephew of Lorenzo the Magnificent.

Giulio's accession was not to be in any way as simple as that,
however. Allied with the Emperor, he faced the pro-French faction
in the Conclave, and there were others with old family axes to
grind against the Medici. The election dragged on for weeks, and
the cardinals were bricked in and put on meagre rations to force
a decision. Giulio's ultimate victory in mid November was seen as
a win for the Emperor and Spain over the French, and laid the
groundwork for new intrigues which would vex Giulio for much of
his pontificate.

He took the name Clement VII and, although as a cardinal
he had served with some distinction as secretary of state under Leo,
virtually from the beginning he was regarded as a well-intentioned
but wavering and indecisive pope. The Venetian ambassador at the
Vatican at the time, Marco Foscari, sketched him in these terms:

'The Pope is forty-eight years old and is a sensible man but
slow in decision, which explains his irresolution in action. He
talks well, he sees everything, but is very timid ... He withdraws no
benefices and does not give them in simony. He gives away nothing,
nor does he bestow the property of others. But he is considered
avaricious ... people grumble in Rome. He gives largely in alms,

but is nevertheless not liked. He is very abstemious, and is a stranger to all luxury. He will not listen to jesters or musicians and never indulges in the chase or any other amusement ... His entire pleasure consists in talking to engineers about waterworks.'[2]

Perhaps it was a hangover from the glory days of Leo, or that simply too much was expected of another Medici. 'With all his good qualities, Clement was weak, hesitant, and always a little late; and he tried to play the old Italian political game in circumstances which no longer permitted it.' In the process, Clement 'made certain of the Protestant schism, and lost England to Rome'.[3]

This latter observation concerns his refusal to annul the marriage of England's Henry VIII to Catherine of Aragon, a matter over which, struggling with the advice of conflicting advisors, he dithered at length. But there was another catastrophe to befall the Church in the time of Clement: the sack of Rome. It may be hard for some to comprehend it now, but less than five centuries ago, Rome and the Vatican, which had survived the depredations of a thousand years of Huns, Vandals, Goths, Visigoths and Saracens, was once again overrun by hostile forces, its people butchered, raped and tortured and its treasures carted off as booty. The difference was that this time the invaders could not be characterised as pagan hordes, but were themselves Christians. How that disaster came to pass is the second instalment of the tragic epic of the Emperor, the King, and the Pope.

✠ ✠ ✠

In late 1524 the French army of Francois I was on the march once more in Italy, intent again upon taking Milan and moving on south to Naples, both with titles to which he considered he had a legal right. Milan fell readily enough, the forces of Emperor Charles V ejected and the French in control. Sensing which way the wind was blowing, Clement threw the support of Rome behind François, on the undertaking that the French would leave the Papal States alone on their march south to Naples.

But Clement had backed the wrong horse. Rather than resting and re-supplying his forces, emboldened with a first taste of victory Francois pressed his men on, and laid siege to the imperial stronghold of Pavia, some thirty or so kilometres south of Milan. A few weeks after the French took Milan, early on the morning of 24 February 1525, the mightiest armies of Christendom clashed head-on outside the city walls of Pavia, Christian cutting down Christian. In an unremittingly brutal clash of cannon and arquebus, sword and pike, entire French units were outmanoeuvred, surrounded and hacked down to a man by the combined Spanish-German army of the Habsburg Emperor. In spite of their numerical superiority, the forces of Francois were routed, with a number of French nobles falling at the head of their troops. The king himself, his horse shot from beneath him, kept fighting on foot until he was surrounded and taken prisoner on the field sodden with the blood of his men. Francois was conveyed back to Madrid and kept prisoner at Charles's pleasure. From there he wrote to his mother Louise, 'all is lost to me save honour and life, which is safe'.

The other loser on that morning in Pavia was a man safely far to the south of the clashing swords, Clement. For the time being, however, Charles resisted any urge to move upon Rome and his former ally, but opted to reach terms with Clement in a new treaty. After a year of captivity, Francois secured his release by pledging his solemn word to Charles that he would desist from his territorial ambitions.[4]

He never had the slightest intention of doing so. Upon his

return to Paris, Francois and Clement entered into yet another treaty, the French king given the Pope's absolution for breaking the vow he had given to Charles. Thus the so-called Holy League of Cognac was formed, with the Pope, France, Venice, Milan and Florence all lined up against the Habsburg emperor: a formidable alliance against a formidable foe.

But Charles faced other, even potentially bigger problems. That same year, 1526, he had to respond to a threat from the east, the Turkish forces of Sulaiman the Magnificent, and for a time it appeared the squabbling between Christian elements would be a serendipitous sideshow to aid the overthrow of Christendom by the Ottoman Muslims. The Christian world received a reprieve, however, when Sulaiman found the supply lines of his advancing troops were overstretched, and was forced to postpone the next critical phase of his western campaign. In doing so, he freed Charles to deal afresh with the French and their allies in Italy.

Pope Clement had continued to dither over which side to take, leading on Francois against Charles and vice versa, in a bizarre ménage à trois which finally cracked the patience of the Emperor. During the winter of 1526 a powerful German force crossed the Alps under the command of seasoned campaigner George Frundsberg, and efforts by Francois failed to halt their advance into Italy. In February 1527, just two years after the Battle of Pavia, another strong Imperial force was assembled in northern Italy, when Frundsberg's army linked up with a Spanish force under the command of the French turncoat, the Duke of Bourbon. They marched on Rome.

Francois promised Clement more troops: they never came. Clement attempted to muster what Italian forces he could against the approaching horde, but gathered scant support. In a last desperate act he tried to bribe the approaching Spanish-German

army, but with its soldiers now straining at the leash at the prospect
of the legendary riches awaiting them in Rome, Clement's offer
was met with contempt. At the last, Clement prayed that the quasi-
mystical power of his office, as the representative of God on earth
and spiritual head of all Christendom, might still deliver him and
Rome from their fate, but his prayers too went unheard.

On the spring morning of 6 May 1527, the Eternal City came
under assault from its attackers. Unfortunately for the Romans
sheltering in their homes from the cannon fire, Frundsberg had
recently died from a stroke and, to make matters worse, the Duke of
Bourbon lay mortally wounded by a Roman sniper. By the time the
meagre defence was thrust aside, a horde of thousands of underpaid
Germans and Spaniards was on the loose within the walls of Rome,
and there was no-one of any real authority remaining at their head
to prevent the orgy of death and pillage that followed.

The Pope was still on his knees praying as the imperial
forces 'stormed the city and sacked it amid such scenes of violence,
murder, rape, looting and destruction that the Sacco di Roma, as
it was called, has remained in the European memory even after
many still more frightful events. The pope fled to the castle of
Sant'Angelo and later to Orvieto ... As for the city, the sack was
rightly seen at the time as the end of a great age. The Rome of the
Renaissance was no more.'[5]

Drunken soldiers menaced the streets, nuns were raped and
priests murdered, palaces and churches pillaged and burned by the
hundreds; nobles were tortured for ransom and hacked to death
if they could not pay. Smoke rose from burnt out buildings and
scavenging dogs gnawed at the rotting limbs of the unburied dead.
As the days and terrible nights passed, the city was given over to a
ghastly carnival of sexual violation and unremitting brutality, an
anarchy befitting depiction by Bruehgel or Bosch.

'A mob of soldiers dressed an ass in bishop's vestments and demanded that a priest should offer it the Host. The man, in last defence of his office, swallowed the wafer himself and was murdered—slowly. Those nuns who were killed after being raped were fortunate, for their sisters were dragged around like animals, to be auctioned off to man after man before finding the relief of death. Luther was proclaimed pope in a mock ceremony. The venerable relics of Rome, the tombs of the popes, were despoiled.'[6]

It was a hammer blow to the Church of Rome delivered by Spanish and German Christians who considered themselves facing a papal anti-Christ, and who used the unfinished Saint Peter's basilica as their stables. Although Charles was said to have been horrified at news of the acts perpetrated by his own men, they would nonetheless occupy Rome for the remainder of that terrible year, and after they finally departed it would take Rome decades to begin to recover. The very spirit of Rome had been shattered: 'After 1527 there was a failure of confidence; and no wonder.'[7]

Clement was flushed out from his hiding place in Orvieto and became a papal itinerant through the Italian countryside, the only persons apparently able to locate him being the English emissaries from Henry VIII still pestering him about his request for a papal annulment of his marriage to Catherine of Aragon. It would seem at the time though that he had other things on his mind, primarily survival.

Imperial forces drove back yet another French incursion in 1528, and the last of the troops of the yet-again defeated Francois were expelled from the Italian peninsula. By the end of 1529 Clement and Charles had come to terms, to some degree at least, offering some prospect of calm. But then a final pair of chickens came home to roost for Clement, ensuring the last years of his papacy and his life would be anything but peaceful.

The matter of the annulment of Henry VIII's marriage had to be settled. Henry, in years gone by styled by the Vatican as the 'Defender of the Faith', was ever more impatient for a positive answer. But Clement was also under pressure from Charles V, whose client he now effectively was, not to grant the annulment, given that Charles and Catherine were relatives.

During the two decades of her marriage to Henry, Catherine became pregnant on several occasions, but suffered miscarriages, still births and infant deaths. The only child to survive was a daughter, Mary. Desperate for a male heir, Henry had asked the Pope to annul the marriage. He had also became infatuated with Anne Boleyn (1500–1536), the dark-eyed sister of one of his mistresses, and wanted to marry her. Clement prevaricated, and a drawn-out crisis grew, the Pope finally ruling against annulment.

When Anne Boleyn fell pregnant in late 1532, the crisis came to a head. The couple secretly married in early 1533, and in May of that year the Archbishop of Canterbury, Thomas Cranmer, ruled Henry and Catherine's marriage to be invalid. The queen was banished to a country estate, where she died three years later.

The Vatican responded with excommunication, and Henry replied with the Act of Supremacy of November 1534, decreeing that the power of the monarch of England within the British realm was absolute. He established the Church of England, formalising a complete break with the Church of Rome.

The split gave further encouragement to the Lutheran movement in Germany and here again Clement, faced with manoeuvrings of Charles on one side and the resurgent Francois on the other, failed to act decisively to prevent a further schism in the Church. But by this time it was probably too late anyway. As the Germans who had sacked the Holy City had shown, there was not much enthusiasm in the north for the kind of Christianity offered by the Vatican and its seemingly endless line of decadent popes.

By the time Clement died in Rome on 25 September 1534, the Medici had occupied the papal throne for two tumultuous decades. Now the One Faith was fractured into pieces, the treasury ransacked and empty, the Holy City had been sacked and its nuns raped and priests murdered, and the papacy itself was subject to the whims of a distant emperor. Leo might have thrown a gay party, but Clement left a very bad hangover.

9. PUNCH, COUNTER-PUNCH AND THE PETTICOAT CARDINAL

I feel much freer now that I am certain
the pope is the Antichrist.

—MARTIN LUTHER

The 75-year-old Paul III who looks out from the famous portrait by Titian might to the contemporary eye appear more like a shepherd than a pope. This is a description a pope might welcome, being the herdsman of God's earthly flock. There is something undeniably bucolic in his bushy moustaches and whispy beard, but to categorise him as a simple *contadino*, or peasant, would be a mistake. Paul III was among the most sophisticated of men ever to have gained the papacy, and in Titian's portrait, painted in 1543, a thoughtful intelligence is manifest in his gaze, along with sensitivity in his long, delicate fingers. Three decades before Titian, the young Raphael had painted the same man, the then youthful Cardinal Alessandro Farnese, and captured the same intelligence in the eyes; but Raphael had noticed something else too, and painted determination in the line of the mouth. Alessandro would one day need all these qualities, and more.

The Church he inherited from the Medici was in dire need of such a man. Its fortunes were at a low ebb. Rome and the Vatican lay ransacked and ruined, the treasury picked bare. England's king Henry VIII had formalised the split in the faith by founding the Church of England. Even bigger trouble brewed in Germany, where Martin Luther and his followers were in open revolt and ready to strike out on their own path.

The way ahead was fraught for everyone, and a drawn-out havoc of murder and mayhem was in the offing in the name of religious belief. As Kenneth Clark put it: 'Fire rains down from heaven on kings, popes, monks and poor families; and those who escape the fire fall victim to the avenging sword. It's a terrible thought that so-called wars of religion, religion of course being used as a pretext for political ambitions, but still providing a sort of emotional dynamo, went on for one hundred and twenty years ...'[1]

Such was the enormity of the storm clouds gathered, and there was little to inspire much confidence in the new pontiff, Paul III. For his contemporaries, even those who had elected him, there was doubt about whether he was up to the task. He was after all the 'Petticoat Cardinal', the nickname he had carried for decades after gaining favour from Alexander VI, when the Borgia pope had Alessandro's sister Giulia Farnese ('La Bella') as his live-in girlfriend in the Vatican. It would take him the rest of his life to live the nickname down.

Alessandro Farnese was born in 1468 in Canino, into a family of nobility with a history as *condottieri*, or mercenary leaders. The territory under the control of his father Luigi Pieri included the important cities of Perugia and Orvieto. His mother, Giovanella, was the daughter of one of the oldest and most venerable aristocratic clans of Rome, the Caetani, descended from popes and princes. Alessandro was educated in the Humanist tradition in Florence and at the University of Pisa, and befriended another young noble, Giovanni de' Medici, later Pope Leo X. Contemporary accounts describe Alessandro as intelligent and thoughtful, a slender young man of medium height, with sensitive features. He was in his mid twenties when in 1493 the newly elected Alexander VI took him under his wing and made him a cardinal, though the tongues of Rome wagged that it was Alessandro's sister who was the pope's real intimate, and the sobriquet 'the Petticoat Cardinal' was coined.

Outgoing, with cultivated tastes in art and scholarship as well as sporting pursuits—all de rigueur for the Renaissance Man—the young cardinal found favour too with Alexander's successor, the imperious Julius II, who rapidly promoted him through various diplomatic posts utilising his rank, intelligence, and charm. He grew rich on his bishopric of Parma as well as his family wealth, and built the elegant and imposing Venetian-style Palazzo Farnese on the Via Giulia in Rome. Despite all these pressing interests he also found the time to strike up a liaison with a cultured mistress, and father four children with her.

In his mature years, at the height of his powers Alessandro served as an invaluable aide to the Medici popes Leo X and Clement VII, but by the time he succeeded the latter in 1534 he was 66 years old and to many eyes a frail and ageing man not expected to occupy the throne for long. Events would prove such impressions wrong, observers missing the strength of determination apparent to Raphael when he painted the younger Alessandro.

'In fact he occupied the Holy See for fifteen strenuous years and saw off a good number of men whom he promoted to the cardinalate. Altogether, he was a much more formidable man than the ever lamenting but rarely lamented Clement: a stubborn, shrewd negotiator, a man who knew his mind, a man of sufficient character to restore both respect and purpose to the papacy. For himself he recognised the justice of the universal complaints against the unreformed Church of Rome and from the first demonstrated his readiness to tackle quite thorny thistles.'[2]

Otherwise variously described as wise and as sly—and in spite of his reforms accused like so many of his predecessors of nepotism, having promoted his son and grandson to positions of influence—the older pontifical Alessandro was more commonly seen as affable and good natured, even magnanimous, gifted as a speaker and a learned conversationalist; and, unlike his predecessor Clement, when a decision had to be made he acted decisively and stood by it. The final summation of him remains complex and contested, however, G.R. Elton arguing the negative:

'... that this subtle, slow, prolix, ailing man pursued too often a devious and discreditable course clean contrary to the interests of his spiritual charge is plain enough and hardly qualifies him for a high place among popes in general. The favourable estimate would seem to rest on what he did for the papacy rather than the Church.'[3]

The major thrust of this criticism seems to stem from his involvement in political matters, his detractors claiming that he was still acting 'like a child of the Renaissance', or some kind of latter-day Julius II. Yet in the time of Paul, matters of politics and those of religion remained very tightly interwoven, and it was almost impossible for any one man—even a pope with the mingled spiritual and temporal authority he still wielded—to unpick one from the other.

✠ ✠ ✠

Like Clement, Paul faced hydra-headed problems, exacerbated in his case by the sullenness that still clung to the blackened stones of the sacked city of Rome. The wounds of 1527 were still keen, the graves of the murdered still fresh. He quickly addressed himself to Rome's historically weak defences, which had allowed the invaders entry with such ease, rebuilding and remodelling the city's fortifications. He re-secured the city's food supply, and sought to lift the mood of the people with carnivals and parades.

But beyond Rome itself, there was a much larger picture which would have daunted anyone, even a man of ability. To the north, Germans arrayed themselves against Rome under the Protestant flag of Luther. To the west, the Holy Roman Emperor Charles V and France's king Francois I, the two sovereign lords of Christendom, remained intractable foes spitting insults and missiles at one another. From the east came the most serious threat of all, the armies and the fleets of the Ottoman Turks of Sulaiman the Magnificent.

It was Sulaiman (1494–1566) the 'Sultan of Sultans', whom the Pope rightly saw as the real foe: all the rest was schoolboy squabbling by comparison. Like Paul, Sulaiman was an educated and thoughtful ruler. During his four and a half decades at the helm of the Ottoman Empire, in addition to his significant territorial gains in military campaigning, he was active at home where he addressed himself to social and legal reforms. He was particularly energetic in the latter, a fact marked by his name in Arabic as *Kanuni*, The Lawgiver. Like Lorenzo, with whom he shared the honorific 'the Magnificent', Sulaiman is considered a cultured Renaissance Man, renowned for his patronage of the arts. He was an energetic builder of palaces, schools and mosques. Some of the Muslim world's architectural masterpieces were designed by his architect, Abdul Mannan Sinan, including Istanbul's Shezade Mosque, now a global landmark.

But it was for his military prowess that Sulaiman was known and feared in the west, and by the time of Paul III he had been on the march for more than a decade. Soon after taking the throne in 1520, Sulaiman led his forces into the Balkans and took Belgrade in 1521, followed by Budapest. Driving all before him, he advanced through Hungary into Austria, reached Vienna and laid siege there in 1529. The siege was ultimately repelled and Sulaiman retreated to Istanbul, but he had threatened the heartland of the western world, and Christendom was on notice.

Sulaiman's men were victorious at sea too, where his fleet—said to be the largest and best equipped in the world at the time—inflicted a heavy defeat on Pope Adrian's forces in the Eastern Mediterranean by capturing Rhodes in 1522. Sulaiman's admiral Khair al-Din Barbarossa continued to menace Malta and the Christian sea lanes, and facilitate Turkish landings on the Italian peninsula itself, which inevitably alarmed the Italian states and Rome.

Such was the man Christian forces found themselves pitted against, yet time and again they found their internecine disputes more pressing, contesting them more hotly and at vast cost in men and materials. Given the absence of united opposition, had Sulaiman not been overstretched by lengthy supply lines, he might have driven a wedge into the heart of Christendom. He was certainly more than capable of it: in addition to his successful campaigns in eastern Europe, he found time to make himself master of Persia and even take Baghdad, the ancient capital which the Ottomans would not relinquish for nearly four centuries, until 1917, towards the close of the First World War.[4]

But while it was plain to Paul that the main military challenge came from the Ottomans, this was anything but obvious to Charles V and Francois I, who continually reignited a personal and imperial quarrel which had already lasted for the better part of a generation. Francois wanted Milan and he wanted Naples: Charles would not cede. The quarrel went on and on, and the personal enmity between the two only ever seemed to grow more bitter and deep. As a contemporary of Francois, the French marshall and military strategist Blaise de Monluc put it: 'God almighty raised up these two great princes sworn enemies to one another and emulous of one another's greatness, an emulation that has cost the lives of 200,000 persons and brought a million families to utter ruin.'[5]

This was the price these twin pillars of the faith expected from their subjects because they coveted each other's titles, territory and prestige: seemingly an attenuated breach of the Tenth Commandment, if not the Deadly Sin of Pride itself. Charles even offered to meet Francois in single combat, a duel to end things, but Francois would have none of that, preferring grandiose military schemings to a simple outcome between the two as men. So problematic for Christendom did their rivalry become that in 1538 Paul journeyed to the disputed city of Nice in the hope of bringing them together to resolve their differences, but again papal intercession proved fruitless. So it went on, for most of the pontificate of Paul, the Pope attempting a delicate neutrality while Charles and Francois continued to court him, each against the other, and Sulaiman watched for his opening.

Paul's other problem—if possible even more chronic—was Germany. Martin Luther's appearance in 1521 before Emperor Charles V at the Diet of Worms[6] had achieved little or nothing of substance: Luther had refused to retract the most inflammatory of his 95 theses, as demanded by Leo X. Despite virtual house arrest, he continued to agitate against Rome, and then scandalised it even more than the likes of Rodrigo Borgia had done before him, by openly marrying. For a clergyman this was rebellion enough, but even more salaciously, his bride, Katharina von Bora, had previously been a nun.

The two were introduced by an artist, the painter Lucas Cranach (the Elder, 1472–1553), who later painted them and served as a propagandist for Luther.[7] If the couple felt any shock wave emanating from Rome at their union, they blithely ignored it and went on to raise a family of five children.

The Peasants Revolt of 1523–25 further destabilised an already complex situation, and the Sack of Rome two years after that complicated matters even more, as did England's formal break with Rome in 1534. During the 1530s Luther's tone became ever more strident and condemnatory, and there appeared little chance of reconciliation. He was set upon an irrevocable path, one in which he foresaw only more profound change to come, from the next generation. As he told students in 1531:

'We old men, soaked in the pestilent doctrine of the papists which we have taken into our very bones and marrow ... cannot even to-day, in the great light of the truth, cast that pernicious opinion out of our minds. For habits acquired in tender years cling with the utmost persistence. But young men like you, your heads still fresh and not infected with such pernicious teaching, will have less difficulty in learning about Christ purely than we that are old in rooting out these blasphemies from our minds.'[8]

The publication of Luther's theses saw another religious reformer from across the border, in Switzerland, following suit. Huldrych Zwingli (1484–1531) came from the Wildhaus region of Toggenburg, in the north-east of the country. Born into humble circumstances, he reached university, studying in Vienna and Basel. After graduation he entered the clergy, becoming a parish priest at Glarus and serving as a chaplain with the Swiss military.

Influenced initially by the reformist notions of Erasmus, he began stating increasingly critical positions about the Church. Like Luther and Erasmus, he was scathing about the sale of indulgences. He began denouncing the Mass, which critics had come to view as little more than a pagan rite, and encouraged the stripping of images from churches, a purge of idolatry.

Though a clergyman, like Luther he married, even if in his case the union was kept discreet at first. In 1523 he brought disaffection with Rome to a head in a public debate in Zurich, a spectacle which seized the imagination of a populus eager to hear matters of doctrine and conduct argued openly. As with other aspects of his life and his thinking, Zwingli is said to have taken his lead from Luther in calling for the debate, following Luther's verbal stoush in Leipzig with the eloquent Catholic defender John Eck.

In the Zurich debate, a crowd of six hundred from each side of the religious divide braved the midwinter cold to gather in the Town Hall on 29 January 1523. Zwingli had prepared his case meticulously, and stage-managed it masterfully. It amounted to a frontal assault on the Church of Rome, its doctrines, rites and conduct, and the papacy.

'Zwingli sat in the centre at the front with his Hebrew, Greek and Latin Bibles open before him. He had prepared Sixty-Seven articles as a basis for discussion. The first fifteen articles state his positive doctrines, what the gospel is, who Christ is, what the

Church is. The remainder constitute his objections to the pope, the mass, intercession of the saints, compulsory fasting, pilgrimages, monastic vows, clerical celibacy, gabbled prayers, indulgences, purgatory and other teachings and practices. The disputation resulted in enthusiastic approval of Zwingli's teachings and an order that all priests of the canton should promote them.'[9]

Zwingli's triumph and the official embrace of his views added new impetus to the Protestant cause across northern Europe. With the blessing of the Swiss people he set himself to the task of changing their religion almost beyond recognition.

'In the years 1523 to 1525 he gradually reformed the whole Church at Zurich, abolishing the mass, introducing vernacular services, embodying his interpretation of scripture in new orders on baptism and communion service ... What made him a radical was his conviction that salvation depends on faith alone and is confined to those whom God has chosen: his idea of the Church was more exclusive than Luther's, and anticipated the narrow and disciplined body of Calvin's Church.'[10]

Like Luther, and Calvin to come, Zwingli found little in common with fellow Protestant reformers. In fact it is fair to say that to some degree at least the differences between the major Protestant leaders played into the hands of the Pope—or might have—giving him a little breathing space by presenting him with less than a united front. Despite efforts such as the Colloquy of Marburg of 1529, Zwingli and Luther failed to join together Swiss and German Protestantism.

Religious fighting in Switzerland was to prove even more a problem, and ultimately fatal to Zwingli personally. Although they had signed a peace treaty, Catholic and Protestant regions came into armed conflict. The Catholic forces prevailed decisively at the Battle of Kappel near Zurich on October 1531 where Zwingli himself was killed: Rome could at least count one adversary fewer.

But a deeper crack soon opened in the once-unified facade of the Church two years after Zwingli's death, with the conversion of French scholar Jean Calvin to the Protestant cause, initiating a new phase in the Reformation.

Calvin (1509–1564) was born a lawyer's son in the town of Noyon in Picardy, about 100 kilometres north of Paris, and was a boy when Luther nailed his theses to the church door in Wittenberg. The serious-minded, highly intelligent young Calvin went on to be educated at the University of Paris, graduating a Master of Arts. While he was drawn towards further studies in theology, his father demanded he change to the financially reassuring study of law. Calvin did as he was told and was on the path to being a lawyer when he found himself drawn to the ideas of Luther and other Protestants. After the death of his father Calvin took the opportunity to give up law and in 1533 revealed his conversion to the Protestant cause.

Jean Calvin was a very different type of man to his fellow Protestants, being '... hostile to scholastic philosophy; unlike Luther, he did not draw his ideas from this traditional reservoir but went straight to scripture, Paul and Augustine, and his whole nature was pragmatic rather than abstract. He never really liked Zwingli, who seemed to him too fond of metaphysical argument where faith alone sufficed.'[11]

Forced underground by Catholic France, Calvin wrote *The Institutes of the Christian Religion*, in which he set down the doctrine of predestination in which some humans are the elect of God to Heaven, while others, no matter how they may live, are doomed. The religion which grew from his ideas was unstintingly puritanical and austere, and became a byword for the most severe and joyless form of Protestantism.

Some scholars have argued that Calvin represented a deeper threat to Rome than Luther, who was more open and demonstrative in his dealings with the papal hierarchy than his French counterpart. Calvinism can also be seen as more of a creed unto itself, doctrinally and certainly emotionally remote from the more exuberant faith as practised in Rome.

Calvin's *Institutes* was published in 1536, and in the same year, in collaboration with William Farel he wrote his *Confession of Faith*, which serves as a summary of his views expressed in the main work.[12] The *Confession* opens with a clarion call which Pope Paul in Rome could only interpret as a gauntlet tossed against his authority:

> *1. The Word of God*
> *First we affirm that we desire to follow Scripture alone as rule of faith and religion, without mixing it with any other thing which might be devised by the opinion of men apart from the Word of God, and without wishing to accept for our spiritual government any other doctrine than what is conveyed to us by the same Word without addition or diminution, according to the command of our Lord.*

The darkness and austerity of Calvinist thought is summarised in two of the articles upon the nature of humanity, and their content and tone could not be in more sombre contrast to Rome and the papal goings-on of recent memory:

> *4. Natural Man*
> *We acknowledge man by nature to be blind, darkened in understanding, and full of corruption and perversity of heart, so that of himself he has no power to be able to comprehend the true knowledge of God as is proper, (nor) to apply himself to good works ...*

5. Man By Himself Is Lost
Since man is naturally (as has been said) deprived and destitute
in himself of all the light of God and of all righteousness, we
acknowledge that by himself he can only expect the wrath and
malediction of God ... [13]

How far distant in the memory of Rome now lay the 'Golden Age'
of Leo, the imperial pomp of Julius, and the antics of Alexander?
In Calvin it encountered a sombre-minded, articulate foe who
did not merely want change, but a different faith and a different
world. Such was the zeal of his puritanical doctrine that given the
opportunity to put it into practice in Geneva, he moved with all
speed towards theocratic rule, banned public entertainments,
and even issued a dress code to the citizenry. Not surprisingly, the
people of Geneva did not stand for it and sent him packing. His
doctrine was taking hold elsewhere though, and a decade later he
was back in Geneva, propagating a faith which would take root in
France, Germany and Holland, and in parts of Britain.

Rome found itself facing yet another complication in its
struggle for survival: reading. The large-scale printing of books
now allowed for the possibility of a freer flow of knowledge and
opinion than had ever before, when manuscripts were laboriously
copied by hand. A few decades after the widespread adoption
of the printing press, Luther and Calvin used it to devastating
effect against a Vatican, which, until then, had possessed virtually
unchallenged control of the written word. The ultimate outcome
of all this went far beyond matters of faith and religion, into
profound cultural change.

'Luther translated the Bible into German ... and so gave
people not only a chance to read Holy Writ for themselves, but

the tools of thought. And the medium of printing was there to make it accessible. The translations of the Bible, by Calvin into French, by Tyndale and Coverdale into English, were crucial in the development of the western mind ...'[14]

During the Middle Ages literacy rates were extremely low— even by the time of the French Revolution only a third of the French people could read and write—and the mass publication of the Bible in translation by Protestants represented a special challenge to Rome, because large numbers of people, keen to read the Bible, would learn to read through translations by Luther and Calvin.

'Bibles, Psalters, pamphlets, and copies of Calvin's *Institutes* poured from the Geneva presses, which at their peak may have been producing as many as 300,000 volumes a year. These books, whether in Latin or the vernacular, recognised no frontiers ... Pedlars and itinerant vendors would carry them along the trade routes of central and western Europe; bales of books mysteriously found their way into the holds of ships; and grubby copies passed surreptitiously from hand to hand.'[15]

Pressed by an increasingly powerful tide of change, Pope Paul still remained hopeful about returning Henry's England, Luther's Germany, the France of Calvin and the Switzerland of Zwingli to the fold, and initiated moves to attempt to redress their grievances. His measures included the suspension of Clement's excommunication of Henry VIII, in the hope of re-opening dialogue with London.

Besides the critical writings of Erasmus and others, there had long been moves for reform within the Church, a Catholic revival which had preceded the Reformation by a century or more. Indeed, whether the Church's own counter-punch to the Reformation can truly even be characterised as a Counter-Reformation at all is debated among historians, as it may already have been underway before the Reformation.[16]

The rising tide of the Reformation also spawned a generation who remained faithful to the Church at its core, however mindful they might have been of the temporal shortcomings of many who had attained its highest offices. These included the articulate and energetic Germans John Eck and John Cochlaeus, Englishmen Thomas More and John Fisher, and the Italian Jacopo Sadoleto.

It was, however, through the rise of new Orders of the Church, accredited by the Pope, that the practices and the popular reputation of the Church began to be revived. These new Orders, the Capuchins as well as the Banabites, the Theatines, the Ursuline nuns and others, devoted themselves to spiritual values, to charitable work among the poor and sick, and to education of the next generation of Catholics.

'They laboured especially among the destitute, diseased and lost masses of Italy, a work of charity deserving the highest praise as much as it fulfilled the highest need.'[17] Nonetheless Orders such as the Capuchins needed powerful friends as they also encountered opposition to their charitable works. 'They naturally excited the usual distrust and dislike felt by the worldly and secure, but also the rational and cool, for uncomfortably sincere and generally rather wild men who find it impossible to hide their conviction of their own rightness behind the forms of proper modesty.'[18]

In other words, a devotion to kindness and care for others went against the grain for many of those who had become accustomed to a Church which fulfilled a different role, of guaranteeing power, wealth and privilege to its ruling elite. Against these now were arrayed men and women who saw the work of the Church not in the silk brocading of papal vestments, but in caring for the sick and the poor—something which could render them dangerously popular. To his credit Paul overrode all opposition, confirming the Capuchin Order in 1536.

But the Pope's most historically important decision by far towards a Counter-Reformation was his confirmation of another new Order, the Society of Jesus, or Jesuits.

✠ ✠ ✠

The Order's founder was a Basque, Iñigo Loyola, better known now as Saint Ignatius Loyola. The youngest son of the aristocratic Loyola family, he was born in the family castle overlooking the town of Azpeitia in Guipuscoa province, about 25 kilometres south-west of the city of San Sebastian. His noble birth gave him entry into the most rarified circles of Spanish society, including the royal court of Isabella and Ferdinand. There he seems to have conducted himself much as one might have expected from a well-born courtier of the time, his demeanour evoked in the precisely calibrated language of the Catholic Encyclopaedia:

'He was affected and extravagant about his hair and dress, consumed with the desire of winning glory, and would seem to have been sometimes involved in those darker intrigues, for which handsome young courtiers too often think themselves licensed. How far he went on the downward course is still unproved. The balance of evidence tends to show that his own subsequent humble confessions of having been a great sinner should not be treated as pious exaggerations.'[19]

It would appear that it was not simple vanity and the pleasures of the flesh which consumed the young Loyola either. He had visions of personal grandeur, initially fed, as with another legendary Spaniard, the Don Quixote of Cervantes, by a voracious appetite for reading the romances of chivalry and knight errantry which were the pulp fiction of his day.[20] The two volumes of Cervantes' masterpiece were written in the decades after the death of Loyola, and accounts of the Jesuit founder's fascination with popular books of knight errantry may well have helped inspire Cervantes, along too with popular accounts of the exploits of the Conquistadors in the New World.[21]

Perhaps dreaming of one day leading an army into battle—a destiny which indeed did await him, although not in any form the preening young dissolute might ever have imagined—Loyola entered military service. His dreams were soon shattered, when at the age of just 29 he was badly wounded in action against the French during their siege of the northern stronghold of Pamplona. Serious enough in itself, the wound was not as terrible as the treatment he would undergo for it.

'... a cannon ball, passing between Ignatius' legs, tore open the left calf and broke the right shin (Whit-Tuesday, 20 May, 1521). With his fall the garrison lost heart and surrendered, but he was well treated by the French and carried on a litter to Loyola, where his leg had to be rebroken and reset, and afterwards a protruding end of the bone was sawn off, and the limb, having been shortened by clumsy setting, was stretched out by weights. All these pains were undergone voluntarily, without uttering a cry or submitting to be bound. But the pain and weakness which followed were so great that the patient began to fail and sink.'[22]

Stricken with a fever, he defied the opinions of his doctors by surviving. What he read during his long recovery induced a life-changing conviction. 'Then, in order to divert the weary hours of convalescence, he asked for the romances of chivalry, his favourite reading, but there were none in the castle, and instead they brought him the lives of Christ and of the saints, and he read them in the same quasi-competitive spirit with which he read the achievements of knights and warriors. "Suppose I were to rival this saint in fasting, that one in endurance, that other in pilgrimages." '23

Fired with such notions during his year of convalescence, in March 1522 he visited the Benedictine monastery of Montserrat in the mountains above Barcelona, where he gave away his rich clothes and hung up his weaponry before an image of the Virgin Mary. He attempted to write a thorough catalogue of his sins—compiling it is said to have taken him three days—and made a full confession.

On his route back to Loyola, he stopped off in the small Catalan city of Manresa, high in the mountains inland from Barcelona. He lived in a cave for eight months where, troubled by lingering doubts about whether he had really managed to catalogue each and every one of his sins, he submitted to a severe self-discipline of deep meditations and prayer, accompanied by bodily privations of cold and fasting. He experienced visions there, a phenomenon which would recur for the rest of his life.

It was also during this period that he accumulated the experiences that would comprise the raw material for *The Spiritual Exercises*, the seminal text which would later become the wellspring of discipline for his educational and missionary agenda.

He decided to undertake a pilgrimage to Palestine, the Holy Land, a journey which in its perils and legendary hardships rivals the travails of Quixote himself, during which Loyola suffered chronic ill-health and near starvation, as well as shipwreck and imprisonment. His terrible ordeal proved all for nought too: under strict orders from the Pope, the Franciscan friars in charge of the holy sites in Jerusalem would not permit Christian pilgrims access for fear that they would be kidnapped and held for ransom by locals. So at the end of a harsh and bitter journey, Loyola had no alternative but to turn around and find sea passage as best he could back to the port of Barcelona.

Perhaps on deck somewhere returning across the Mediterranean, or in the period soon after his return to Spain, he began the transition from mystic pilgrim to spiritual leader. Armed with his experiences in the cave in Manresa, which he was inscribing into the *Spiritual Exercises*, he glimpsed a means to draw a group of like-minded Catholics around him in a highly disciplined religious cadre. His preparations for his calling included studies at a number of universities, one of them Salamanca, Spain's finest, though this increasingly odd-seeming noble could not help but attract the eyes of officialdom.

'All this time, though still a layman, he attracted attention by a life of severe holiness and found himself giving spiritual counsel to troubled souls, mostly women. Not unnaturally, this brought him to the notice of the Inquisition, since both his unauthorised ministry and the character of his group (which included both noblewomen and ex-prostitutes, both given to manifestations of hysteria [sic]) raised totally unfounded suspicions of heterodoxy and immorality.'[24]

Loyola was briefly imprisoned before being cleared of all suspicion and in 1527 moved to Paris. There he undertook further studies, survived more dire poverty and sickness, and rejected the growing Protestant trend. He was fortunate to escape a public flogging for an alleged breach of college discipline when his college principal listened to his version of events and gave him the benefit of the doubt. During his Paris years he gathered a small band of followers, including Francisco Xavier, who would in years to come be canonised as Saint Francis Xavier. Loyola's Paris group of seven comprised the core of what would soon be the Jesuit Order, and he trained them through the disciplines in his book *Spiritual Exercises*.[25]

'On the face of it, the work is neither very original nor very inspiring ... it possesses a total air of practicality, a kind of sober obviousness in an essentially mystic setting which is the secret of its impact on those who for several centuries have come to it prepared to listen and to follow. In form it consists of a detailed and precise course of meditation and study ... which the aspirant must undergo in strict sequence and total obedience to the instructor. The student searches his soul for sins and defects, in the process acquires the means for ridding himself of them, meditates on Christ and His passion, and is quite literally made over. The evidence is overwhelming that many who have undergone this training felt themselves to be new men, possessed of a moral strength and capacity for religious experience which they did not know until Spiritual Exercises called forth the resources of their souls. The pedagogic purpose and success are equally patent: St. Ignatius' relationship to his disciple is that of teacher and pupil—even drill-sergeant and recruit—rather than of mystical visionary and follower.'[26]

On 15 August 1534 the group of seven assembled in Montmartre where they all took vows of poverty and chastity, as well as to journey to the Holy Land to undertake missionary work there—and to put themselves at the disposal of the pope. Paul III did not know know it—he was not even pope yet—but the vows Loyola and his followers took that summer would provide him and popes to come with sworn followers who would form a Catholic bulwark against the Reformation, who would teach the young of the Catholic realm to read and write, and would fan out across the world recruiting new faithful in vast numbers from the four corners of the earth, extending the influence of the Catholic Church and the papacy beyond even the worst nightmares of any Luther or Calvin.

By 1537 the group was in Venice, awaiting transport to Palestine, but the way was blocked by Turkish fleets patrolling the

Mediterranean. Their options thinning, the group undertook ordination to the priesthood in Venice and then moved south towards Rome, to fulfil their vow to place themselves at the disposal of the pope.

The little band was just a few miles short of Rome when Loyola experienced a vision which he interpreted as foretelling the blessing of Jesus Christ on their enterprise and from that point on the group had its name, the Society of Jesus.

Loyola drafted the articles of the order, which included the resolution 'to fight under the banner of God in our Society, which we wish to designate with the name of Jesus, and who are willing to serve solely God and his vicar on earth.' Its goals were 'propagation of the faith by the ministry of the Word, by spiritual exercises, and by works of charity', as well as 'teaching Christianity to children and the uneducated'.[27]

Thus, from the very outset the fundamental objectives of the Jesuits were clearly inscribed: total allegiance to the pope, missionary evangelism, and education. The pyramid of unswerving allegiance was not confined to the pope at the top, however, with the members of the new Order swearing total obedience to their general, and to serve as 'the Pope's soldiers'.

The Papal Court was not exactly agog at the potential of the little group of travellers when they presented themselves at the Vatican. Arguments for and against ran through the curia for official approval of the new Order, with powerful Cardinal Guidiccioni arguing against, but another powerbroker, Cardinal Contarini, arguing for them. Although Pope Paul himself publicly favoured approbation, Guidiccioni briefly held sway. With approval initially refused, Loyola and his followers redoubled their efforts. Perhaps sensing which way the wind was blowing, Guidiccioni gave way, and on 27 September 1540 Paul issued the Bull *Regimini militantis Ecclesiae*, approving the founding of the Jesuit Order. No other single act of any pope would have such a significant and enduring effect to reinforce the core strength of the Roman Catholic Church.

Although its numbers were initially restricted to 60—the caveat was removed after two years—the Society of Jesus would quickly grow in size and influence, to become one of the most potent entities within the Church. Against his declared wishes, his followers drafted Loyola as the first General in 1541. His war injuries and health were, as ever, troublesome, and the workload onerous. After several years in the post he attempted to resign, but his followers would have none of it, and he remained at the head of the Jesuits for a decade and a half, during which the society's first missionaries undertook initial work in the Americas, India and Africa.

Early missionaries included Saint Francis Borgia (1510–1572), the great grandson of Rodrigo Borgia, Pope Alexander VI. A personal friend of Loyola's, Francis Borgia undertook missionary work in the Americas and later rose to become General of the Jesuits. The society also attracted those, like Loyola himself, who wished to escape from what they felt was a sullied past:

> The Portuguese Inacio de Azevedo was the son of a priest, the grandson of a bishop, the son and grandson of nuns. When he learned of his birth, he held it to be a fourfold sacrilege, believed himself called to a life of sacrificial reparation, joined the Society of Jesus and its Brazilian mission, and was murdered by pirates in the mid-Atlantic.[28]

What then is the final judgement of history upon such a man as Ignatius Loyola? Reformation historian Elton is exacting in his judgement, calling him

... one of the most remarkable but also strange personalities of that age or any other. Short, slight, racked by illness, permanently lame after his wound at Pamplona, of limited intelligence and never a scholar, preacher or theologian, Loyola hardly looked an inspiring figure. His passion for system and planning often deteriorated into pedantry and pettifogging regulation. Although he was from his young days addicted to fantasies, substituting after 1521 dreams of knightly service of Christ for dreams of knightly service to ladies without at first seeing any essential difference between the two, his imagination was always rather meagre; he entirely lacked all poetry in the soul. The visions which came to him so frequently during the last thirty-five years of his life, and which he learned to turn off and on at will, were nearly always of the simplest kind—mere phenomena of light such as discs or rays, all of which he unhesitatingly identified as some specific manifestation of the divine. Though, therefore, a mystic, he was the coolest visionary that ever thought himself directly inspired by God.[29]

Despite the seeming toughness of such a judgement, an authentic understanding shafts through it: Loyola was indeed a dreamer, one inspired to a quixotic quest, though not to a damsel shrouded in muslin, but a man in white. He endured extraordinary privations, even if many of them were self-inflicted, of poverty, of illness, of anguish before officialdom. He took a tiny band of men on an impossible journey to Jerusalem but they ended up, perhaps unsurprisingly, in Rome, the capital of Christendom, and succeeded in his goal there.

The worst of his privations sprang from a simple 'quid agendum'—what to do with this life? As such he was not an abnormal man at all, but a very normal one—who, after all, has not asked themselves that question, searchingly and often?—and a man who literally did follow his dream, no matter how strange or hopeless it got, to the end.

On the way he gained the unquestioning devotion of followers in whom Pope Paul glimpsed the promise of something very worthwhile. In an era when a sworn treaty could last a week and the loyalty of soldiers could not be counted upon after payday, if at all, where princes swapped sides with the insouciant treachery of well-skilled players of the board game Diplomacy, here instead were men whose deepest desire was to serve the pope in whatever manner he saw fit. They were the pope's own men, his to rely upon.

Paul's judgement to accept them and their vow of loyalty to him, and to the popes who followed, was vindicated a thousandfold by their successes in starting to educate the vast and illiterate Catholic peasantry of Europe so that they might at least know what they believed in, instead of what they were told by clerical shysters and pedlars of indulgences; and by journeying far afield, literally widening the front against the Reformation, outflanking it with missionary conversions of native Americans, Indians and others in their so many thousands, and then their many millions. The Jesuits took the struggle far from the old battlegrounds of Europe, to help re-draw the map of the Christian world, and in the process reshape history. What man better to start all that than a lame Spanish dreamer, and who better to give him the chance than a shrewd old Italian?

✝ ✝ ✝

All the while that Loyola and his men had been coalescing into the core of what would become the Jesuits, Pope Paul had been laying the groundwork for the other great thrust of the Counter-Reformation, a Council of the Church where the challenge of the

Reformation could be dealt with directly and forthrightly, all the issues properly aired and solutions sought.

But in attempting to set up the Council, the Pope once again ran foul of the deja vu machinations of the Charles-Francois rivalry, a web in which, no matter how he might struggle to free himself, he remained enmeshed. Their rivalry played itself out yet again in Paul's long, though ultimately successful campaign, simply to summon a Council. As far back as 1518 Luther himself had pleaded the case for a Council as the only way to deal with the grave matters he had raised in his Theses—and in the certain knowledge that if he were to journey to Rome to debate his views, he would be incinerated as a heretic.

Because of the complexity of the larger political situation prior to and inevitably after the 1527 Sack of Rome, and in spite of numerous attempts, Paul's predecessor Clement had failed to summon such a Council, and Protestant sentiment had been allowed to grow ever deeper and more virulent, take root and spread. Despite an inevitable sense that he may have been shutting the stable door years after the horse had bolted, Paul was nonetheless intent upon calling a Council to consider the grievances of Luther and others, some of which he and the more liberal-minded Church leaders considered reasonable, and see what might yet be salvaged. Paul made it a priority of his papacy, acting soon after taking the throne by repeatedly urging the cardinals to the calling of a Council.

His preparations included a realistic look at the Church and its conduct, and commissioning a report into past abuses, such as lapses within various Orders, the accumulation by senior clergy of unseemly wealth by dubious means, improper or at the very least highly inadequate procedures for the ordination of the clergy, and other practices which had scandalised much of the Christian world.

Unfortunately for Paul, his attempt to examine what had been going on went awry when Protestants got hold of the report, and it became live ammunition for Luther from his pulpit in the north. Here after all was the Church's own evidence of its malfeasances and deep-rooted corruption.

Paul encountered predictable difficulty in attempting to get Charles and Francois into any accord on the Council's agenda— as well of course as the cardinals and bishops, and the various potentates and petty despots dotted through Christendom.

His efforts began in earnest in mid 1536 with an attempt to set up a Council in Mantua. There were inevitable delays and stalling, particularly from Charles, who continually accused the Pope of siding with Francois against him, even though Paul protested a steadfast neutrality. The task would have tested the patience of Job, but Paul persisted with it, employing his gift for diplomacy to coax the many feuding factions toward the table to talk. The enmity between Charles and Francois remained yet an intractable stumbling block, and this deep and long-running sore was about to become even more problematic.

In 1535 Francois secretly sent an envoy to the Turks and held talks with Sulaiman's admiral Khair al-Din Barbarossa. It was in many ways a reckless and destructive move—some scholars even consider it the critical moment of the abandonment of the very concept of Christendom. The Turks responded favourably and Francois enjoyed Sulaiman's aid against Charles in the Italian peninsula and the Western Mediterranean in 1542 when a combined Christian and Moslem force was pitted against the Habsburg army of the Holy Roman Empire. Although no formal treaty had been signed between the king and the sultan, Turks and French fought side by side in the Siege of Nice in 1543, against an alliance of Habsburg and English troops, Charles having managed to conjure an ally of his own in the Protestant (and now sick and ageing) Henry VIII of England.

After decades of jealous and bitter personal struggle between Charles and Francois, the situation had now degenerated into a brawl in which Catholics, Protestants and Moslems gave their lives in indecisive battles and bloody skirmishes, all of which only served to drain wealth from the combatant sovereigns, the prosperity from their kingdoms, and trust, hope and life from their subjects.

The situation was apparently resolved in 1544 with the Treaty of Crépy, when Francois (yet again finally) agreed to relinquish his territorial ambitions in Italy. Francois had now spent the best part of his life in this fruitless military pursuit, but his fighting days were not quite done yet, and he campaigned one more time to expel the English troops of Henry VIII from France.

The Charles-Francois rivalry ended forever with the death of Francois on 31 March 1547—according to some accounts in his last days still dreaming about a yet another Italian campaign, while complaining about the burden of the crown God had placed upon his head. His adversary Henry VIII was already dead by then, the news of the English monarch's passing initially filling the Frenchman with good spirits.

'Early in 1547, during a ball at Saint-Germain, the King received news that Henry VIII had died on 28 January. According to the Imperial Ambassador, Francois "laughed loudly and joked with the ladies". His mood changed when he remembered how the Englishman had recently reminded him that "they were both mortal". From then on Francois became "more thoughtful than hitherto".'[30]

According to accounts from the period, on the same night he received the news of Henry's death, Francois fell ill with a fever. He tried to shake it off, but his courtiers privately remarked upon his worryingly changed, unhealthy appearance, and bouts of fever persisted, accompanied by abcesses.

Less than two months after Henry's death, Francois took to his bed, never to rise, his last words 'Jesus, Jesus'. His lust for territory, and his profound abiding bitterness at not getting all that he wanted, had literally eaten him out. 'When the doctors opened his body they found an abcess in the stomach, his kidneys shrivelled, his entrails putrefied, his throat corroded, and one of his lungs in shreds.'[31] So was the 'Prince of the Renaissance', when he died at the age of 52.

Henry VIII had been in little better state, if not much worse, when his time had come. The first sovereign to formalise a break with Rome—not in his case over doctrinal disputation or clerical misbehaviour, but for want of women and sons—he had squandered the love of the English people to become a despised tyrant. Grown hideously obese in middle age—he is reputed to have attained the proportions of three large men by the end—his heath deteriorated in his mid fifties. He suffered horribly from leg ulcers which developed into gangrene, and some accounts attest to the ulcers bursting open and a 'horrendous stench' as he died. Even worse in some regards, his coffin came open during the transportation of his body from London to Windsor for burial, and dogs were found licking his corpse—a less than illustrious end for another Renaissance Man.

Like most of the others in the epic conflict, Martin Luther's health had been severely sapped by the years of argument, discord and fighting, and he had long suffered from bladder and kidney problems, fainting fits and, towards the end, angina. His deteriorating health made him ever more irascible, and his noted anti-semitism surfaced in a final vitriolic attack on the Jews in his last days, when he is said to have preached for their expulsion from Germany.

Luther died in February 1546, Henry VIII in January 1547 and Francois in March 1547. In the space of thirteen months, three of the key cast members of the Reformation drama were dead. When the corpses were removed from the stage, only Charles V and Pope Paul III were left standing, with Sulaiman, as ever, watching from the wings.

Now, after nearly a decade of waiting, Paul was at last able to convene his long-cherished Council, in the northern Italian city of Trento, or Trent, on 13 December 1545. Strategically at the foot of the Dolomites and south of the Swiss border, Trent was also proximate to the major players in the Reformation—Germany, France and Switzerland. Sessions went on there for nearly four years, despite Paul's efforts to move the Council south to the relative safety of Bologna following a plague scare, and rumours of imminent attack by Protestants.

There was still difficulty between Emperor and Pope. While Charles wished to press forward on matters of behaviour and discipline, Paul also promoted consideration of doctrinal matters. As for allaying the fears and addressing the concerns of Protestants, it was simply too late now, with the Reformation entrenched in an arc across northern Europe. Whether things would have turned out differently had there not been years of petty impediments to convening the Council, is an historically interesting speculation, although it would appear that by the time Paul gained the papacy the Church had passed the point of no return with a great multitude of followers who had simply lost faith in it.

Yet, in his own way, Paul III did achieve a lasting victory over Protestantism, of a kind. In 1546, more than four decades after Julius II had approved Donato Bramante's design for the new Saint Peter's Basilica, Paul summoned the now 70-year-old grand old man of the Renaissance, Michelangelo Buonarroti.

The two knew each other well: Michelangelo had painted the frescoes of his Pauline Chapel, as well as *The Last Judgement*. The task he now set the aged Michelangelo was to re-design the incomplete Saint Peter's.

Michelangelo complied, and in the process designed the elegant dome, the tallest in the world, the pièce de résistance of the biggest church in the Christian world, and today one of its best known and loved features. It was also a powerful reply to all those who had wished to strip churches of all their beauty and ornamentation, people for whom human artistry seemingly had no place or worth. The dome Michelangelo created ran exactly counter to such puritan austerity, an eloquent and resounding re-assertion of the values of the Renaissance.

The immense task of constructing Saint Peters, the labour of decades on the money pit of Rome, was now assured of completion. It may have almost bankrupted the Church, the indulgences to build it may have hurried on the Reformation, looting soldiers may have stabled their horses within its walls, and its completion still decades off; but it would be finished. It would become a place of worship matchless in the Christian world, stewarded by a man once maligned as having stolen into the halls of power in the petticoats of his sister, a man with a quiet determination not to be deterred, as Raphael had discerned.

Not long after the suspension of the Council of Trent in September 1549, like Francois I who had shared (and sometimes prompted) his travails, Paul III fell ill with a fever. It came upon him in the first week of November and he died a few days later on 10 November 1549, aged 81. In his last confession on his death bed, he repented his nepotism.

Had he known what was coming, he might well have repented another of his acts, establishing the Roman Inquisition. In 1542 he had placed Cardinal Gian Pietro Carafa in charge of it—a harsh, inflexible man who before long would himself be seated upon the papal throne—and equipped him with sweeping powers to 'imprison on suspicion, to confiscate property, and to execute the guilty'.[32] A new and terrible time had arrived for the people of Rome.

10. THE HARDMAN PONTIFF

A defence in the Inquisition is of little use to the prisoner, for a suspicion only is deemed sufficient cause of condemnation, and the greater his wealth the greater his danger.

—JOHN FOXE, AUTHOR OF *FOXE'S BOOK OF MARTYRS*

by the time of the death of Paul III, the Catholic communities of Europe could have been forgiven for suffering crisis fatigue. They had been through the halcyon days of popes Alexander VI, Julius II and Leo X, the disintegration of Rome's power under Clement VII and the sack of the Holy City, then Paul III's attempts to get to grips with Luther and the Reformation, the imperialist designs of the Ottomans, and the destructive drawn-out rivalry between the Holy Roman Emperor and the King of France. By the time Julius III was elected pontiff in 1550 after more than six decades of chaos, many would have been grateful just for a period of calm to take stock. And that is what, to an extent, they got.

The man who would assume the title of Pope Julius III was a Roman by birth, born Giammaria Ciocchi del Monte in 1487.

His father was a successful lawyer and he set out to follow in his footsteps, studying law until he turned to theology. His advancement in the Church was rapid, succeeding his uncle to become Bishop of Siponto in 1512 and being appointed Bishop of Pavia in 1520 when he was still only 33. A few years later he faced his sternest test when he was handed over to the occupying Germans as a hostage during the sack of Rome. Fears that the occupiers of Rome intended to kill the young bishop led to an audacious and successful plan by Cardinal Colonna to free him. Made a cardinal himself in 1536, he became co-president of the Council of Trent when it convened in 1545.

When the cardinals met after the death of Paul III in 1549, del Monte was an obvious frontrunner, but powerful factions favoured other candidates including the English cardinal Reginald Pole, who had himself co-presided at Trent. In the end Del Monte became the compromise candidate, and was elected on 7 February 1550.

Although some of his appetites may have surprised his fellows,[1] he got down to business by reconvening the Council of Trent. He was intent on curbing the financial excesses of the cardinals and urging discipline upon the monastic orders, but infighting forced him to suspend it in April 1551. He forged a neutral position between the French and Habsburgs, whose rivalry yet persisted. He became a strong supporter of the Jesuits and granted the Society an annual subsidy from the Vatican coffers.

Perhaps the most important event during his pontificate had little to do with any direct action of his own: the return of England to the Catholic fold after Queen Mary I took the throne. Mary was the daughter of Henry VIII and Catherine of Aragon, the annulment of whose union Henry had sought so keenly, and the denial of which precipitated his split from Rome. Mary gained the throne after the attempt by the Duke of Northumberland to have his daughter-in-law Lady Jane Grey crowned queen of England.

The failed plot of the 'Nine Day Queen' was in some respects one of the most tragic episodes in the history of the British monarchy. Renowned for her beauty and intelligence, the 27-year-old Jane was also very well connected: the daughter of the Duke of Suffolk, her grandmother was a sister of Henry VIII. Her father-in-law, John Dudley, the Duke of Northumberland, was eager to exploit her links to the royal family and so deny the throne to the Roman Catholic Mary. When the young King Edward VI was on his deathbed, Northumberland alleged that he had named Lady Jane as his successor. So it was that the young woman unwittingly found herself at the centre of a desperate plot involving key figures of the English nobility.

Jane arrived, still unaware that Edward had died and grew even more confused when two nobles knelt and kissed her hand. She blushed, embarrassed as they referred to her their sovereign lady. And still she stood confused; for she could not bring herself to believe that such a cataclysmic event as Edward's death could have been hid from her, his cousin and the general public. Lady Grey was then led into the Chamber of State, in a rather formal procession, where Dudley led her to a dais reserved for royalty. Jane looked on in continued confusion as the assembled group, including her parents, paid homage to her. Dudley then came forward and gave a lengthy speech in which Jane finally learned of Edward's death and eventually ended with the declaration that Edward's death wish had been for Jane to take the throne after him. Jane stood there trembling and later wrote that the moment left her 'stupefied and troubled'. She was speechless. They all knelt yet again to her and she swayed and fell, breaking into sobbing tears. No attempt was made to help her stand, nor to soothe the tears. Among her sobs the words 'Such a noble prince' were heard. Finally,

she regained enough control to utter the words, 'The crown is not my
right and pleaseth me not. The Lady Mary is the rightful heir.'[2]

Urged and cajoled by male courtiers to take the crown, she repeatedly refused to allow it to be placed on her head, only relenting to 'see how it fitted'. Emperor Charles V was informed of her taking the throne, as were the people of London, but with many of them in mourning for the deceased king there was little celebration in the city. Mary had refused to renounce her cause and, despite an expressed desire to avoid bloodshed, marched on London at the head of an ever-growing army. The Duke of Northumberland could only muster a motley militia of a few hundred, and with the cause lost, man by man the nobility slipped away from the young woman's side, abandoning her to her fate. Trumpet blasts announced the arrival of Mary, and Jane was taken captive and imprisoned in the Tower of London as the bells of London rang out for the rightful queen. During that July of 1553, Jane had ruled for nine days, the shortest reign in English history.

Another attempted plot by Jane's hapless male supporters prompted Queen Mary to sign her death warrant. On a chilly winter's day in February 1554 she was taken from her cell in the Tower. She had already seen the corpse of her beheaded husband, Lord Guildford Dudley, being taken from a cart, and knew only too well what awaited her. She was blindfolded and laid her head on the chopping block, asking her executioner as she felt for the block 'What shall I do? Where is it?' before the axe fell, beheading her for treason. According to the tradition, her severed head was lifted and brandished aloft, the words proclaimed: 'So perish all the Queen's enemies! Behold, the head of a traitor!'

The sad tale of Lady Jane took root in English consciousness, especially after the eventual Protestant triumph. A few decades after her execution, Shakespeare wrote: 'the sun, for sadness, would not show its head', while more than two centuries after her death, the author, artist and illustrator William Hone (1780–1842) extolled her virtues and condemned the squandering of her life by her male relatives.[3] Lady Jane Grey remains something of a feminist cause celebre today, a tragic and unwilling victim to grasping male vainglory.[4]

While few in Rome would have been much discomfited at the death of the young Protestant, the accession of a Roman Catholic queen to the English throne was cause for loud rejoicing. At the news of Mary's coronation, Pope Julius dispatched ambassadors to London to assist in the long hoped-for Catholic restoration, but he did not live to see the long-cherished dream of England's return to the Catholic fold. Before his envoys set foot on English shores, Julius was dead and a new and dangerously turbulent chapter was about to open for the papacy, Rome, and the Catholic world.

First, however, there was the brief interregnum of Marcello Cervini degli Spannochi (1501–1555), who was elected pope in April 1555. Like the Dutchman Adrian of Utrecht four decades before him, Marcello decided to retain his own name, becoming Pope Marcellus II—and also like Pope Adrian, his was destined to be one of the less conspicuous papacies: Marcellus occupied the office for only 22 days. A committed reformer, he is said to have thrown himself into the massive task with such zeal that, combined with the exertions of Easter Week services, he was left exhausted. Though by no means an elderly man by the standards of the papacy—he was in his mid fifties—he fell sick and died. He is commemorated in the sung mass, *the Missa Papae Marcelli*, by the great composer of liturgical music, Giovanni Pierluigi da Palestrina.

His death cleared the way for a nobleman from one of the aristocratic families of Naples, Gian Pietro Carafa (1476–1559).

From an early age he had been the nepotic beneficiary of the largesse of his uncle, Cardinal Olivero Carafa, at the time one of the most powerful of the cardinals. He introduced the young Carafa to the court of Alexander VI while Gian Pietro was still in his teens, and his advancement was rapid thereafter. He represented Leo X in England and Spain, but his time in Spain left him with a deep distaste of Spanish influence throughout the Catholic realm, and their possession of his home city of Naples had long stuck in his craw, as it had with many Neapolitans.

An ascetic from an early age, the tendency only deepened in his maturing years, when he resigned his comfortable posts and joined a new religious Order which would gain the name of the Theatines after Carafa, who was also known as 'Theatinus'. Like a number of the new Orders which sprang up during the Counter-Reformation, the Theatines were known for their severity and austerity, and strict vow of poverty. These were properties which suited Carafa, and he rose to the rank of General. His severity marked him as the right man for the hard work needed for the Counter-Reformation, and Paul III empowered him towards ecclesiastical reforms. He was made a cardinal in 1536, later the Archbishop of Naples, and placed in charge of the Roman Inquisition, a post which made him one of the most feared men in Europe.

The cardinals gathered in the spring of 1555. As was usual, strong factions were at work behind the scenes. The now aged Carafa (he was nearing eighty) considered his own candidature unlikely, noting 'I have never conferred a favour on a human being', but he garnered support. Given Carafa's known antipathy to Spain, it was hardly surprising that Emperor Charles V attempted to veto his election, but failed, and on 23 May 1555 the man born into Neapolitan nobility became pope and took the name Paul IV.

The kind of man he was may be glimpsed from his tomb sculpture by Pirro Ligorio in the church of Santa Maria sopra Minerva in Rome. The long, bearded face appears strong and determined, but also severe and uncompromising. This was certainly how he ran his papacy: his election struck fear into the hearts of even the most courageous.

'While Ignatius Loyola was still a theological student in Paris, Carafa had denounced him as a heretic, and Ignatius 'trembled in every bone' when he heard of the Cardinal's election.'[5]

Elton's opinion of Carafa is in many ways as exacting as his view of Loyola.

'(Paul IV) had always been a violent and unrelenting man, and now he was filled with an old man's etched-in hatreds. Above all he hated the Spaniards who ruled his native land of Naples. He therefore hated the Jesuits, many of them Spaniards and certainly dominated by Spanish ideas of Christianity, nor had he ever forgiven Loyola his tactless letter criticising the Theatines. He seriously considered abolishing the Order and put a temporary stop to its successful expansion and missionary activities; only the death of Ignatius in 1556 and the election of Lainez, who for some reason could get along with the pope, saved the Society.'[6]

However, some saw more positive aspects. 'A more severe discipline was introduced into the churches. All begging was forbidden. Even the collection of alms for masses, which had previously been made by the clergy, was discontinued, and pictures whose subjects were not appropriate to the Church were removed. A medal was struck in his honour, representing Christ driving the money changers from the Temple. Monks who had left their monasteries were expelled from the city and from the Papal States. The court was enjoined to keep the regular fasts; and all were commanded to solemnise Easter by receiving Holy Communion.

The cardinals were even compelled to do occasional preaching; Paul himself preached. Many abuses profitable to the curia he did his best to correct. He would hear no talk of marriage dispensations, or of the resources which they furnished to the treasury. A host of positions which, up to his time, had been regularly sold, even the Clerkships of the Chamber (chiericati de camera), he would now allow to be assigned only by merit.'[7]

This commitment to reforming the Church and to addressing himself to divisive doctrinal matters can be seen from the earliest pronouncements of Paul IV. A few months after taking the throne, in August of 1555, he made it an article of faith that Mary, the mother of Jesus, 'was a virgin before, during, and after the conception and birth of her son'. With the stroke of a quill he had settled, in his own mind at least and as such in the minds of all his millions of followers, a debate that had been going on for centuries, and his view has abided.

But it was on the political front, and dealing with the wider issues of the Reformation, where his uncompromising character was to be most tellingly tested. He had scarcely been pope for six months when he formed another new alliance with the French in yet another attempt to push the Spanish and the Habsburgs out of Naples. As with virtually all other schemes against the Habsburgs, it ended in disaster with defeat at the hands of Imperial and Spanish forces in August 1557. At the command of the Catholic Queen Mary, English forces under Lord Pembroke joined on the Spanish side and a major battle took place at Saint-Quentin in northern France. The French were routed and their commander, Constable de Montmorency (like Francois I before him), captured. The overwhelming victory prompted the Spanish king Phillip II to order construction of the massive granite monastery of El Escorial in the Guadarrama mountains outside Madrid.

With the French in disarray, the Spanish began another push on Rome, under the command of Fernando Álvarez de Toledo, the Duke of Alba. He was among the most proficient (and feared) military commanders of the sixteenth century, and the prospect of the 'Iron Duke' marching on Rome at the head of another Spanish army must have instilled intermingled feelings of fear and hatred in the mind of Pope Paul. Lest Rome be exposed to another sacking at the hands of Spaniards, the Pope agreed to terms, even though his virulent antipathy towards all things Habsburg and Spanish remained undimmed.

Citing lack of papal approval beforehand, he even refused to recognise the abdication of Charles V and the election of his brother Ferdinand I as Holy Roman Emperor. After four decades of fighting and religious chaos in Europe, Charles retired to a monastery at Yuste in northern Spain, where he shortly died in 1558. His son Phillip gained the crowns of Spain and the Netherlands, already the husband of England's Queen Mary. The Catholic world had a rare chance for reconciliation and unity. But Pope Paul's undimmed animosity against the Spanish would remain a stumbling block.

✠　✠　✠

Perhaps even more harmful to the Church than any acts of Paul IV were his decisions pertaining to England and Reginald Pole (1500–1558). Born in Staffordshire into the nobility and a cousin of King Henry VIII, Pole was educated at Oxford and blossomed into a gifted Humanist scholar, his writings drawing the attention of other great minds of the era such as Thomas More and Erasmus.

Crisis fissured Pole's life when his friend and kinsman Henry VIII sought his support and offered boons including the archbishopric of York, to help obtain the much desired annulment of his marriage to Catherine of Aragon. Pole is said to have spoken to him with such candour that in a fury Henry almost drew his dagger on him. Pole remained publicly discreet about his opposition to the annulment, and in 1532 withdrew to further studies abroad in Padua. Later, politely resisting orders from Henry to return home to now Protestant England, he accepted an invitation from Pope Paul III to live in Rome, where he was made a cardinal in 1536.

After Pole was commissioned by Paul to attempt to unite Catholic Europe against Henry, the English king replied with demands and threats. There were rumours he had sent assassins to murder his erstwhile friend, given credence when Henry signed the death warrant of Pole's mother, the Countess of Salisbury, and she was executed.

Pole distinguished himself further by co-presiding over the Council of Trent. At the Conclave of Cardinals after the death of Paul III in 1549 it appeared for a time that the Englishman had the numbers to become pope, until support ebbed away to Cardinal del Monte, Julius III.

After the accession of Queen Mary to the English throne in 1553, Pole was dispatched to England as papal legate. He was received with great ceremony in London, absolving Parliament of any guilt from the Protestant breakaway. He was well received at court and on good terms with Mary and her husband Phillip, and succeeded Thomas Cranmer as Archbishop of Canterbury.

What should have been a time of triumph for Catholic England turned to catastrophe, however, in the fingers of Pope Paul. Furious at Pole's attempts to broker peace between France and the Habsburgs when the anti-Spanish pontiff craved anything but that, Paul turned with a vengeance on the man who presented the best hope for the full restoration of Roman Catholicism to England. Paul voiced doubts regarding the doctrinal orthodoxy of the liberal and scholarly Pole, his legateship was cancelled, and Pole was recalled to face the Roman Inquisition.

He ignored the order, but personally shattered at the loss of a great opportunity, died in London on 17 November 1558. On the same day in the same city, the other great hope of Catholic England, Queen Mary, also died. Pope Paul then rejected the claim of Princess Elizabeth to the crown—Mary's half-sister was the daughter of Anne Boleyn—but she ascended the throne anyway, and under her English Protestantism reasserted itself. Queen Elizabeth I (1533–1603) reigned for four and a half decades, into the next century, by which time any chance of returning England to the fold of Rome appeared long gone.

The harsh and ham-fisted mistreatment of Pole, and of other liberal-minded reformers such as the jailed Cardinal Morone, represented a clear opportunity let slip, a new start squandered. A creator of the Counter-Reformation, the hard and impetuous Paul IV almost single-handedly wrecked it too.

✛ ✛ ✛

If the legacy of Paul IV were not clouded enough by his belligerent politics, futile battles and maladroit handling of England, his name is also indelibly linked with the Inquisition. The Inquisition[8] dates back three centuries before Paul to Pope Gregory IX, who set it up in 1231 against a backdrop of concerns about heresy, but also witchcraft, sorcery and alchemy and other occult practices returning with the Crusaders from Palestine. That the Church decided it needed such a severe response to heresy indicates that even back in the thirteenth century there were concerns the Church was starting to lose its sway over Europe.

A complex procedure of interrogation which gave the accused the opportunity to recant and seek forgiveness, but not to speak in their own defence, the Inquisition soon acquired an even darker hue when torture was authorised by Pope Innocent IV in 1252. Now the accused could be literally grilled by the inquisitor until they confessed, reaching a theatrical climax with the auto-da-fé:

> The ultimate decision was usually pronounced with solemn ceremonial at the sermo generalis—or auto-da-fé (act of faith), as it was later called. One or two days prior to this sermo everyone concerned had the charges read to him again briefly, and in the vernacular; the evening before he was told where and when to appear to hear the verdict. The sermo, a short discourse or exhortation, began very early in the morning; then followed the swearing in of the secular officials, who were made to vow obedience to the inquisitor in all things pertaining to the suppression of heresy. Then regularly followed the so-called 'decrees of mercy' (i.e. commutations, mitigations, and remission of previously imposed penalties), and finally due punishments were assigned to the guilty, after their offences had been again enumerated. This announcement began with the minor punishments, and went on to the most severe, (i.e., perpetual imprisonment or death). Thereupon the guilty were turned over to the civil power, and with this act the sermo generalis closed, and the inquisitional proceedings were at an end.[9]

Those who had confessed under torture inevitably confessed anything their torturers asked of them—as might be expected on the rack, or at the end of a red hot iron—and they were led away to prison or to the stake to be burned. Their wealth was then confiscated and divided between the Inquisition and the Church, adding an enticing financial incentive to the discovery and burning of ever-larger numbers of heretics and witches.

This is not to say the use of torture was new in the court procedures of Europe. The Greeks had permitted it in some circumstances and the Romans had inevitably taken a leaf from their book, although it was strongly opposed by some of the most thoughtful and eloquent of ancient Rome, including the orator Cicero and the philosopher Seneca.

In twelfth and thirteenth century Europe, torture was put to increasingly common use in pursuing self-incriminating testimony, to put an accusation putatively beyond doubt. Its use would persist for hundreds of years up to the Enlightenment, in the wake of which it appears gradually to have subsided in Europe. It would reappear in the twentieth century, however, in interrogation procedures of the Nazis and others including the Cambodian dictator Pol Pot and various military juntas, and in the twenty-first, when the United States employed methods of torture to attempt to extract information from suspected Islamic terrorists and others.

Human beings have long shown an aptitude for inducing pain in one another, inflicting tortures from the irritating to the excruciating. Methods have ranged from branding with irons and ripping out nails and teeth, to the rack which stretches the spine of the agonised victim to breaking point. The Iron Maiden was a human-sized box which when closed upon the victim pierced their body with steel points while preventing their screams from being heard outside, while sharp-pointed thumbscrews had a similar affect on a smaller scale.

There were instruments specially designed for use against

women including 'breast-rippers', and 'The Pear'. This latter definitively cruel device, used against women accused of sexual union with the Devil, was a metal contraption which was forcibly inserted into the victim's vagina before being screwed open, inducing throes of agony. Another device was 'Jock's Mare' a sharp instrument which the victim was forced to sit upon and 'ride', the untreated wounds resulting in gangrene of the rectum. Methods more recently in vogue with torturers include electrodes inducing electric shocks to the genitals, the US-sanctioned practices of 'waterboarding' or near-drowning, and psychological tortures including sleep deprivation and mock execution.[10]

As the Mediaeval Inquisition deepened in severity, the papacy decided that torture was no longer adequate to its needs and approved the death penalty for accused heretics—a sentence carried out by secular authorities so that the fingers of the Church would not be sullied with the flesh of those it consigned to be charred at the stake. As the practice spread, 'witches'—in many cases women whose sole offence was speaking their minds, or being heir to a valuable property—were burnt, hanged, strangled and drowned in their tens of thousands,[11] as were large baskets of cats burned as 'familiars' of Satan.[12]

While the Church disputes any notion that it was solely responsible for the frenzy of witch burnings in Europe during the Middle Ages—and it is plain that witches had been targeted back into pre-Christian antiquity in an ongoing conflict between traditional beliefs and organised religions—it cannot be denied the Church played a central role in how events unfolded. Pope Innocent VIII's 1484 Bull *Summis desiderantes affectibus*[13] fuelled the mediaeval mania for burning witches. While the *Catholic Encyclopaedia* seeks to minimise the influence of Innocent's Bull, it does concede that his recognition of the existence of a supernatural reality peopled by 'witches' meant that life was much more perilous for any unfortunate women who might fall into the clutches of inquisitors and lynch-mobs.

> *Indirectly, however, by specifying the evil practices charged against the witches—for example their intercourse with incubi and succubi, their interference with the parturition of women and animals, the damage they did to cattle and the fruits of the earth, their power and malice in the infliction of pain and disease, the hindrance caused to men in their conjugal relations, and the witches' repudiation of the faith of their baptism — the pope must no doubt be considered to affirm the reality of these alleged phenomena ...*[14]

To the illiterate peasantry of Europe, official sanction of the real existence of such fantasies—given by their trusted spiritual leaders, among the best educated and most highly privileged people of the time—was a direct incitement. Now, whenever their crops failed, their cattle fell sick or they suffered impotence, it could well be the doing of a witch. They had a Papal Bull telling them so, and they knew how the Church dealt with witches—it burnt them alive. And that is what mobs set out to do across Europe, burn witches, the vast majority of them women.

'Probably the most disastrous episode was the publication ... of the book *Malleus Maleficarum* (Hammer of Witches). This work is divided into three parts, the first two of which deal with the reality of witchcraft as established by the Bible etc., as well as its nature and horrors and the manner of dealing with it, while the third lays down practical rules for procedure whether the trial be conducted in an ecclesiastical or a secular court ... the *Malleus* professed (in part fraudulently) to have been approved by the University of Cologne, and it was sensational in the stigma it attached to witchcraft as a worse crime than heresy and in its notable animus against the female sex.'[15]

According to comparative religion scholar David Chidester, the *Malleus Maleficarum*, written by two Dominican inquisitors, Jacob Sprenger and Heinrich Kramer, became the 'primary guide to witch-hunting'.[16]

The imagination and temper of Europe's peasantry had long been fired by lurid descriptions of the rites and revels of these so-called witches. Accounts melded images of pagans (adherents of the 'Old Religion', retaining pre-Christian pantheistic beliefs and ritual practices), herbalists, soothsayers and the like, with the black magic practitioners of a 'cult of Satan', the Devil himself. Chidester summarises the sensationalist popular accounts of the time from his reading of the *Malleus Maleficarum*:

> At these nocturnal meetings, the Devil appeared in the form of a cat, a toad, a duck, a goose, a man with goat's legs, or a black man to receive the devotion of witches who took turns kissing him on the buttocks. After a ceremonial meal of disgusting food, the witches engaged in an orgy of heterosexual and homosexual intercourse. Any children that might be born from this sexual activity were supposedly eaten eight days after birth. Their pact with the Devil, however, enabled witches to fly through the air, change shape, acquire material wealth, and cause harm to others by secret means. The stereotype of diabolical witchcraft, therefore, contained features of the traditional image of the witch with the notion that witches were the supreme heretics, the adherents of a secret, underground organisation, the Church of Satan.[17]

Though some in the modern Church might argue the finer points, few could raise much real doubt regarding its complicity in the so-called 'Burning Times'—a complicity fostered in part by its ongoing determination for tight centralised authority and control, and fed by misogyny. The Inquisition and the craze for burnings which grew from it stand as crimes against humanity by the Church and papacy, which did not move against it but, as we have seen above, fostered it and allowed it to spread and become entrenched.

'Between 1427 and 1486, witch-hunting flourished in Northern Italy and southern Germany, as local inquisitions were established to identify witches and turn them over to secular authorities for execution. During the following three centuries, as local witch-hunts developed throughout Europe, an estimated 100,000 people—80 per cent women—were killed as witches.'[18]

The *Catholic Encyclopaedia* is at pains to spread the blame around, however, noting that such deeds were not confined to Roman Catholics:

> One fact which is absolutely certain is that, so far as Luther, Calvin, and their followers were concerned, the popular belief in the power of the Devil as exercised through witchcraft and other magic practices was developed beyond all measure ... In 1572 Augustus of Saxony imposed the penalty of burning for witchcraft of every kind, including simple fortunetelling. On the whole, greater activity in hunting down witches was shown in the Protestant districts of Germany than in the Catholic provinces ... In Osnabrück in 1583, 121 persons were burned in three months. At Wolfenbuttenl in 1593 as many as ten witches were often burned in one day.[19]

A new dark era began with the setting up of the Spanish Inquisition in the latter part of the fifteenth century. Following the defeat of the Moors and their expulsion from Spain, the kingdoms of Castille and Aragon sought and gained papal approval for an inquisition to root out heretical Moriscos and Marranos—Muslim and Jewish converts to Christianity—who were said to be plotting to subvert re-conquered Christian Spain.

The man who approved the establishment of the Spanish Inquisition was Pope Sixtus IV, in 1478. The hands of Sixtus were already bloodied, having that same year promoted a violent plot to overthrow the Medici.[20] The Spanish established the Inquisition in Seville, but so brutal were its outrages that within a few years Sixtus attempted to shut it down, without success. Having taken root, the Inquisition would not be given up easily by its Spanish enthusiasts. The Pope was pressured and cajoled into appointing a Grand Inquisitor to oversee the entire inquisitorial machinery, and the first to occupy the post was the tyrannical monk, Tomas de Torquemada (1420–1498).

The nephew of a Dominican cardinal, Torquemada was born in Valladolid and joined the Dominican Order as a young man. At the age of 32 he was appointed prior of the monastery of Santa Cruz in Segovia, and became confessor and confidante to Queen Isabella. After Pope Sixtus appointed him Grand Inquisitor in 1483, he promptly extended his jurisdiction over wide swathes of Spain, from Madrid to Mallorca, Zaragoza to Valencia. He also moved to extend greatly the range of offences for which a person could be hauled before the inquisition, from heresy and apostasy to many other activities and behaviours such as usury, blasphemy, polygamy and sodomy. He licensed his agents to torture victims, and as word spread of his malign activities, the name Torquemada wrought dread throughout Spain. His reign of terror is thought to have led to the burning at the stake of at least 2000 people, and severe injury to thousands more. There were also very many others whose property and life savings were confiscated for the coffers of the Inquisition, and Rome.

Like many others of his time, Torquemada was virulently anti-Semitic, prevailing upon Isabella and Ferdinand to expel all Jews who had not taken a Christian conversion, an order which saw more than 150,000 Jewish people forced to leave Spain. Large numbers fled hostile Europe altogether for the Spanish colonies in the New World where, tragically, they once again found themselves subject to persecution from the Inquisition, when an offshoot of it took root in the Americas.

In his later years, Torquemada's pronouncements and actions became so extreme that a fellow Spaniard, Pope Alexander VI, was forced to appoint a small group of assistant inquisitors to hold him back from his worst outrages. Torquemada's abiding legacy is a name linked in perpetuity with bigotry and horror.

As noted above, the *Catholic Encyclopaedia* remains at pains to minimise the responsibility of the Church for the Inquisition and where possible apportion blame elsewhere, especially for the worst excesses. 'It is to be noted that torture was most cruelly used, where the inquisitors were most exposed to the pressure of civil authority ... Blessed Joan of Arc could not have been sent to the stake as a heretic and a recalcitrant, if her judges had not been tools of English policy. And the excesses of the Spanish Inquisition are largely due to the fact that in its administration civil purposes overshadowed the ecclesiastical. ... Most of the punishments that were properly speaking inquisitional were not inhuman, either by their nature or by the manner of their infliction ... On the whole, the Inquisition was humanely conducted.'[21]

But the *Catholic Encyclopedia* does not question, as it well might, why a religion, avowedly of compassion and charity, was torturing and executing people in their many thousands, because the views of the victims about the virgin birth or the trinity, or the ornamentation of a church or other doctrinal or procedural matters, were not considered adequately orthodox. The question is not asked because it invites the response that whenever the totalitarian control of the mediaeval Church was questioned, it reacted with intimidation, violence and terror. The Church's fear of challenge, of discussion about anything which might undermine its authority or diminish its wealth and power, begat the anger that heated the irons of the torturers of the Inquisition.

✣　✣　✣

Pope Paul IV was responsible for a new and more frightening phase of the Inquisition when he activated the Roman Inquisition, resulting in excesses which became notorious.

'Above all other institutions, he favoured the Inquisition ... The days appointed for Signatura and the consistory he would often allow to pass unnoticed, but never did he miss a Thursday, the day set aside for the Congregation of the Inquisition to assemble before him. He wished the powers of this office to be exercised with the utmost rigour. He assigned new classes of offences to its jurisdiction, and conferred on it the barbarous prerogative of applying torture for the detection of accomplices. He permitted no respect of persons.'[22]

Accounts from the time speak of 'almost a reign of terror in the city. 'Even if my own father were a heretic,' said the Pope, 'I would gather the wood to burn him.' He next turned his attention to works of art commissioned by his esteemed predecessors, entrusting Daniel of Volterra (who was thereafter nicknamed the Trouserer) with the task of clothing some of the nakedness of the Sistine Chapel.'[23]

Among other authoritarian measures, Paul attempted to control the flow of knowledge. Alarmed at the spread of ideas other than its own, the Church had long sought to censor literature, although this became much more difficult after the invention of the printing press and with the mass circulation of books. Paul IV instituted the 'Index Librorum Prohibitorum', or list of banned books.

'Since Pope Leo X's prohibition of 1520 on the dissemination and reading of Lutheran-tainted literature, individual universities like Louvain and the Sorbonne had issued their own lists of forbidden books. The Spanish Inquisition issued its first Index in 1546, and the famous Placards or edicts published in the Netherlands in 1550 by Charles V prohibited the reading, copying or dissemination of heretical literature on pain of death. Now in the late 1550s, still tighter restrictions were introduced. A few months after Luis de Ortiz had written his treatise, the Regent of Spain issued a pragmatic forbidding the import of foreign books, and ordering that all books printed in Spain should in future be licensed by the Council of Castile. The first papal Index, that of Paul IV, appeared in 1559, and the Spanish Inquisition published in the same year, for home consumption, a new and more severe Index of its own.'[24]

While the imposition of the Index might seem something of a lesser evil in a time of so much warfare and cruelty, the ban went to absurd lengths, even to books of grammar, because they had been written by Erasmus (who, despite the bite of his satires, had lived and died a faithful Catholic).

'The *Decameron* of Boccaccio was upon the list ... all the works of Erasmus without exception ... King Henry VIII, Staupitz, Machiavelli, Rabelais, Peter Abelard, and even two editions of the Koran were found upon this eccentric list. It caused a great burning of books throughout Italy ...'[25]

Perhaps the most unfortunate aspect of Paul's Index was that with the precedent set for banning books, the Church felt itself at liberty to tell its millions of faithful what they could and could not read, and order them not to read certain works, under pain of mortal sin. This practice persisted from Paul's time through the many centuries to the contemporary era, with authors such as James Joyce and D.H. Lawrence banned to Catholics in recent decades.

Paul IV also endorsed a ghetto for Rome's Jewish people. Jewish people had long been subjected to the animosity of many others in mediaeval and late mediaeval Europe. Like other peoples such as the Celts and the Huns, they had made a lengthy migration into Europe. Originating in west Asia, where they differentiated themselves from Arabs on religious and cultural grounds, they migrated north into regions such as Russia and south through the Mediterranean, settling in large numbers in Spain.

There they became part of the warp and weft of Spanish society: places such as Toledo now boast centuries-long tolerance and cooperation between the three major constituent communities, Christians, Moslems and Jews. But Jews remained an identifiable ethnic group within the wider society and, as such, as the German dictator Adolf Hitler rediscovered centuries later, were an easy scapegoat for any ills a society as a whole might be suffering.

Jews had long faced entrenched hatred. As we have seen, the fanatic Torquemada urged their expulsion from Spain and Isabella and Ferdinand obliged; Martin Luther advocated the expulsion of the Jews from Germany; and Pope Paul IV enforced a ghetto for Jews in Rome.

While there is considerable debate among scholars, with some arguing he did it 'for their own good', to protect them, and the argument put that cities such as Venice had ghettos for Jews too[26], others see Paul's actions as far less benign. According to Duffy, 'The Jews of Rome were herded into ghettos, forced to sell their property to Christians, and made to wear yellow headgear; copies of the Talmud were searched out and burned.' He goes on to remark there was also a 'campaign to imprison prostitutes, and beggars were expelled from Rome.'[27] This latter campaign was destined to fail given the sheer scale of prostitution in the Holy City, with estimates of up to a third of the population connected with prostitution.[28] A successor of Paul IV, Pius V (pope 1566–72), another grimly ascetic pontiff, took the mistreatment of Jews a step further, expelling them from the Papal States in 1569.[29]

✠ ✠ ✠

To some, Paul IV was foolishly led by bitterness and hatred to steps which permanently harmed the Church through the loss of England, while to others he was the hardline uncompromising leader Rome needed after so many years of corruption, vice and turmoil. There are points in common, however, which we may attempt to draw together into a final image of the man Carafa, Pope Paul IV.

According to the *Catholic Encyclopaedia*: 'He could boast that no day passed without seeing a new decree or reform. He made the Inquisition a powerful engine of government, and was no respecter of persons. The great Cardinal Morone was brought before the tribunal on suspicion of heresy and committed to prison ... The pontificate of Paul IV was a great disappointment. He who at the beginning was honoured by a public statue, lived to see it thrown down and mutilated by the hostile populace.'[30]

Duffy's judgement is that despite his zeal, his status as a real reformer was undermined by his own nepotism: 'It is the supreme irony of Paul's papacy that he should have placed absolute trust in [his] nephews, and both of them abused his trust to line their pockets, a situation everyone in Rome knew about except the Pope. When he finally grasped the true situation, in January 1559, it broke him. He stripped his nephews of all their offices and drove them from the city, but never recovered his confidence or drive, and within a year he was dead.'[31]

In the judgement of Duffy, Paul ended his days a definitively tragic figure, who despite 'unflinching courage and integrity' had failed because of a narrowness of vision, and was ultimately scorned by the people of Rome.

'He was the most hated Pope of the century, and when he died no-one mourned him. Joyful mobs rampaged through the streets of Rome, his statues were toppled and smashed, and the cells of the Inquisition broken open to release the prisoners.'[32]

Perhaps the hardest view of all of this hard man belongs to Elton: 'In his character—his severity, anger at all weakness and corruption, faith in the reformed Church—Paul was the first true pope of the Counter-Reformation; in his politics and attitudes he nearly destroyed it. Only charity, to which even popes are entitled, can suppress the conviction that he was to all intents insane throughout his pontificate. His death came just in time, but it also closed an era.'[33]

II. OLD POPES AND NEW WORLDS

*Gold is a wonderful thing! Whoever owns it is
lord of all he wants. With gold it is even
possible to open for souls the way to paradise!*

—CHRISTOPHER COLUMBUS

The words of Columbus, uttered a decade after his first sighting of the continent of America,[1] reflect the confusion in the Renaissance mind between El Dorado, the fabled city of gold, and the popular vision of heaven. Through the agency of Cortes, the Pizarros and other Spanish Catholic soldier-adventurers, the two notions became interwoven so seamlessly that the slaughter of the native peoples of the Americas and the pillaging of their wealth became a 'holy work' of sorts, entailing the saving of native American souls before their prompt dispatch to God in heaven and the taking of all they possessed on earth.

It would appear on the face of it that a line of credit the size of the Americas could not have come at a more opportune time for Rome. By the time of Columbus the papacy had presided over the Catholic Church for one and a half millennia, making it a most venerable human institution. But the challenges the popes faced at the time of the Conquistadors were many, varied and complex. They included the chronic intrigues of emperors and kings; the Protestant Reformation and the ongoing Inquisition; the leeching of wealth to the sovereign states and the banks; and the penumbra of the approaching Enlightenment in the writings of More, Erasmus and Montaigne, and the theories of scientists such as Copernicus, Kepler and Galileo.

In the sixteenth century the Church and papal power were in a period of evolution towards their present form. The papacy had begun to undergo a process similar to Europe's other absolute monarchs, a gradual ebbing away of real temporal power, to a remnant largely of spectacle and symbolism. Where once popes could consign those they wished to the flames or have their flesh seared with irons, now they were on a path downwards to wielding moral authority alone. Even by the sixteenth century, although there is evidence they might have wished to prevent it, they were powerless to stop the rape of the Americas, and during the centuries that would follow it, little more than wardrobe would be left to the papal drama.

The century had opened promisingly. The death of the wanton Alexander VI in 1503 had opened the way for the militantly assertive Julius II, who expanded the papal territories and filled the treasury, ushering in a golden era which would last for two decades. Construction of the grandest building in Christendom, Saint Peter's basilica, was underway, and the genius of artists such as Michelangelo and Raphael celebrated Catholicism in works of enduring beauty. And then there was the New World, the fantastic, newly glimpsed realm which promised riches beyond imagining for Catholic Spain, and surely something too for Rome, and for all the Catholic world.

The opposite occurred. Spain kept its plunder much to itself and the Vatican went begging, near destitute. With Christendom plunged into yet another round of conflict and chaos that lasted most of the century, in a few decades much of the initial wealth of the New World would be dissipated, spent, and Spain itself broke. Native Americans had died in their multitudes, worked to death by Christians through whose fingers their stolen gold slipped like so much sand. It was not so much the wine in the chalice that was poisoned, as the gold of the chalice itself.

The problem with history, as has been observed, is that it takes so long. Occasionally though it happens almost in a moment. This was the case in 1492, when a pope stood centrestage as the curtain parted on what has been called the greatest single event in human history, the sighting by Europeans of the Americas. The pope was Rodrigo Borgia, Pope Alexander VI, and though a Spaniard, in his position as pope it had fallen to him to divide the spoils of the New World between the two greatest maritime powers of the era, Spain and Portugal. To avoid conflict between the Iberian powers, it was decided that Spain could exploit all that it found to the west of a line north-south down the mid Atlantic, while Portugal could take all to the east of it. In brokering the agreement, the pope in effect poured oil on what might otherwise have become a very troubled Atlantic.

'Alexander may have favoured his native Spain, but his intercession was a statesmanlike determination of a knotty problem that allowed the exploration, which no pope could have stopped in any case, to go on without warfare between two important Christian kingdoms ... The pope saw exploration as a glorious means to evangelise pagans, spreading Christ's gospel, but he intended to do this by good works and preaching ... not by the sword.'[2]

How deeply Alexander really felt such good intentions is open to question, but any contrary views from the Vatican about the conduct of the conquest of the Americas were ignored anyway. By the time the New World was opened up, the word of any pope, devalued by years of scandal and unsavoury practices, weighed little against gold in the scales. Probably it would always have been thus anyway, no matter what.

The Treaty of Tordesillas was duly drawn up and signed in June 1494, and the world was effectively divided in two at the stroke of the pen of a pope. A dramatic papal act had set the stage for the sixteenth century, just as another equally dramatic one—and far more terrible—would bring it to a close. In between lay ten decades of tumult, confusion and death.

✠　✠　✠

When the grandparents of Holy Roman Emperor Charles V, Isabella and Ferdinand of Spain, financed the 1492 expedition of the Genoese navigator Christopher Columbus, the objective was to find a westward route to India and its wealth and spices. What Columbus, nor anyone else for that matter, was that the continent of America intervened between him and his goal. Making landfall and believing they had arrived in India, the Spaniards dubbed the native Americans 'Indians'.

'... that was what Columbus believed [on his return to Spain]. His gold was indeed gold, if in no great quantity, and his parrots were indeed parrots, albeit if not of any Asian variety. Likewise his Indians—the six bewildered individuals who shuffled forward to be inspected by the assembled company were not Indians but Caribs, a race soon to be exterminated by the Spanish colonisers, and, deadlier still, by the germs they carried. The misnomer Columbus conferred has long outlived the conception.'[3]

Although there can be no doubt about the appeal of the natural and man-made resources of the Americas, the Spanish Conquistadors[4] who followed Columbus took what they wanted not for greed alone, but through a calculated blending of greed and missionary zeal. 'The New World had been entrusted by God to the special care of the Kings of Spain, in order that its heathen inhabitants might be brought to an understanding of the True Faith; and, with the obligation, went also the reward, in the form of the gold and silver which these God-given lands were producing in such gratifying quantities.'[5]

While the rulers of Spain might have been grateful for such a bounty, and grasped it, this is not to say Rome endorsed the acts committed by the Spanish in the Americas. There is evidence the popes tried to mitigate against the cruelty of the Conquistadors and the colonists who enslaved indigenous populations to work the silver mines. 'It is to the credit of the Popes of the Counter-Reformation that they steadily condemned the doctrine of slavery for the Indians.'[6]

But who was listening to popes when there was unimaginable wealth for the taking? Against the hunger for gold and silver, for untold riches in a far-off world, the views of the popes counted for little.[7]

The tragedy of one man was to have huge ramifications for the gold and silver the Spanish coveted. He was the Aztec king Moctezuma II, ruler of an empire of 10 million people covering much of modern Mexico and stretching south to Guatemala. In 1519 Moctezuma met the conquistador Hernan Cortes. Cortes had risen from humble beginnings in Medellin, in the province of Extremadura in western Spain. He embarked for the New World to a government post in Hispaniola, and a decade and a half later headed an expedition into the Yucatan Peninsula. Spurred on by tales of the gold and other treasures of the Aztecs, he marched on their capital Tenochtitlan (now Mexico City) toting the gun and the cross, intent on claiming the kingdom for God and Spain.

'In Mexico, Cortes, with his finely tuned irony, told the Aztecs that he and his men "suffered from a disease of the heart which is only cured by gold." Cieza de Leon was inspired to sail to Peru after seeing the Inca gold unloaded in Seville: "As long as I live I cannot get it out of my mind."' All of which perplexed—and, in the end, disgusted—the native peoples. 'The half-Inca historian Waman Poma portrayed an Indian asking a Spaniard: "Do you actually eat this gold?" And the Spaniard replies, "Yes, we certainly do!" The last of the great Incas, Manco himself, bitterly remarked, "Even if the snows of the Andes turned to gold still they would not be satisfied."'[8]

Cortes took up with an indigenous woman called Malintzin, known to history as Malinche. Talented with languages, she was initially his translator, then his advisor in battles against other rival tribes and peoples, and gained repute as Cortes's 'Lover, mistress, concubine, whore.'[9]

Much about Malinche remains a mystery, but this is not the case with Cortes: 'We know little of Malinche's sexual history, but quite a lot about Cortes's, for long before Malinche was ever heard of he was already notorious for his promiscuity, and long after her death his notoriety would continue. In Cuba, for example, where he had lived for fifteen years before launching his expedition to the mainland, there had been persistent scandal ... Bernal Diaz referred to all this in his memoirs. He admired his commander, but he was no fool and saw his faults too. He admitted that he had heard Cortes was "dissolute with women" and "addicted to women in excess, and jealous in guarding his own." '[10]

This is not to say that Cortes, like many other Spanish Conquistadors, did not at least behave like a pious Catholic. '... [Cortes] was devoted to the Virgin Mary, and always kept a statuette of her upon his person, said his prayers and attended mass daily ...'[11]

The help of Malinche would be invaluable to Cortes in his campaign to conquer Mexico, but his final success hinged on a combination of other factors as well. These included the belief of the Aztecs in the coming of a god with a white skin which would herald the downfall of their civilisation, the bringing in of exotic diseases to which the Aztecs had no immunity, Cortes's talent to divide and conquer, a lack of qualms about treachery and murder, and brute firepower, cannon law.

An early account of the strange and awesome weaponry of the approaching Spaniards was given to Moctezuma by a messenger, reported in the mid-sixteenth century Florentine Codex.

'When [the cannon] is fired, a thing like a stone ball comes out of its entrails, raining fire and shooting sparks. And the smoke that comes out of it has a foul smell, like rotten mud, which assaults the brain. If it is fired ... at a tree, it shatters the tree into splinters—an extraordinary sight, as if someone blew the tree apart from within. Their weapons and equipment are all made of iron. They dress in iron; they wear iron helmets on their heads; their swords are iron; their bows are iron; their shields are iron; their spears are iron. Their "deer" carry them on their backs, and these beasts are tall as a roof. Their bodies are covered everywhere; only their faces can be seen. They are very white, as if made of lime ... Their dogs are huge, with flat waving ears and long, dangling tongues. They have fiery, blazing eyes ...'[12]

Not surprisingly, reports like this filled Moctezuma with fear, and ultimately despair. When the two met, unfortunately for Moctezuma everything about him spoke to Cortes of vast wealth, of the exotic, and of plunder ripe for a Conquistador—even his favourite drink.[13]

Cortes tricked and kidnapped Moctezuma, who later died in suspicious circumstances, and the template was set for a conquest through guile and brutality. 'Cortes sent the citizens of Cholula in Mexico a demand that they should recognise his authority and accept the Christian faith ... he murdered more than 3,000 of them, the killing taking more than two hours.'[14]

Within three years Cortes had overthrown the Aztec Empire and installed himself as ruler of the newest province of Spain. He and his men embarked on a wholesale plunder of Aztec wealth, which was shipped in gold and artefacts back across the Atlantic to Spain.

In August 1520, the artist Albrecht Durer visited the palace of Holy Roman Emperor Charles V and marvelled at the newly arrived booty of Cortes. 'I saw the things which had been brought to the King from the new land of gold, a sun all of gold a full fathom broad, and a moon all of silver of the same size, also two rooms of the armour of the people there, with all manner of wondrous weapons, harness, spears, extraordinary clothing, beds and all manner of wonderful objects of human use, much better than seeing prodigies. These things are all so precious they are valued at 100,000 florins. All the days of my life I have seen nothing that touches my heart so much as these things, for I saw amongst them wonderful works of art, and I marvelled at the subtle ingenia of men in foreign lands.'[15]

Of even greater value over time than the precious metals and artefacts were the other items that would transform life around the world forever after, foods such as potatoes, tomatoes, avocados and chillies, exotic flowers, spices and tobacco, and the chocolate which gained rapid popularity in Europe.[16]

Native peoples from the Americas were also freighted back to Europe, and they became the subject of intense curiosity. '... Cortes transported Mexican ball-players and jugglers to perform before the king in Seville. Later they went to Rome and "juggled a log with their feet ... before a delighted Pope" [Leo X]. In Paris, Amazonian Indians acted out their forest lives in circus shows; a Brazilian chief was presented to Henry VIII, and an Eskimo man and woman, from Baffin Island, impressed Londoners with their dignified bearing and modesty.'[17]

It was this dignity of the native peoples of the Americas, however, as well as their wealth, which was under frantic assault, and within a decade of meeting Cortes and his band, many Aztecs were reduced to dogma-parroting mine slaves of Spain. There were voices raised from the beginning against the barbarous treatment of the native peoples, but they were few, and their ultimate effect limited.

'... [Dominican Friar] Antonio de Montesinos ... told his appalled congregation that they were living in mortal sin because of their treatment of the Indians. "Are they not men? Do they not have rational souls? Are you not obliged to love them as you do yourselves? On what authority have you waged a detestable war against these people?"'[18]

When the colonial authorities protested to Madrid about his sermons, rather than waiting to be sent home, Montesinos returned of his own volition and argued the case before the king.

His efforts and those of others like him helped bring about the Laws of Burgos of 1512, which laid down standards for the treatment of the indigenous peoples of the Americas. They were to be made Christians, giving them protection which could not otherwise be guaranteed to people whom the Spanish regarded as savages.

'Natives who worked for wages were not to be ill-treated. Every town was to have an inspector to ensure that the settlers conducted themselves humanely. There were some less philanthropic provisions. The *naturales* (natives) were forbidden to dance. Church-going was compulsory. Old houses were to be burned, to prevent sentimentality. A third of all Indians were to work in the mines.'[19]

Despite the cruelty which native peoples suffered, there are those too who feel the downfall of the Aztecs was inevitable, because of their own brutal practices.[20] Whatever the case, within a few years of the arrival of Cortes, Mexico and its people were subject to Spain.

✠ ✠ ✠

The Conquistadors returning home to Spain took back astounding tales of even more colossal wealth which was ripe for the taking. Glittering horizons beckoned the next wave of Spaniards embarking in Seville for the New World, among them a pig farmer from Trujillo named Francisco Pizarro, who would one day emulate the feats of Cortes by overthrowing the Inca Empire in Peru.

The Inca Empire was the most expansive and best integrated pre-Columbian society in the New World, inhabited by an estimated 6 million people, in a realm stretching from modern Ecuador and Peru down into Chile and the western regions of Bolivia and Argentina. Incas were highly skilled engineers and architects.

They constructed massive mortar-less stone walls, and built and maintained a vast system of roads and bridges, some of them in harsh conditions in the high passes of the Andes Mountains. Their agriculture involved large-scale terracing to boost production, and they had a well-organised administrative bureaucracy.

They also had a large army, but it proved of little use against Pizarro after he managed, like Cortes with Moctezuma a decade before, to capture the Inca emperor Atahualpa and demand that his people fill a large room to the brim with gold. When the Incas complied and the ransom was paid, Pizarro had Atahualpa murdered anyway.

'… Atahualpa was strangled after a judicial murder trial, the penalty of burning alive being commuted because, while the faggots were being piled round his stake, he allowed himself to be baptised.'[21] Many other such 'conversions' were carried out in the same peremptory manner, under duress.

Demoralised by the loss of their leader and subjected to continuing intrigues, betrayals and setbacks, the Incas went from soldiers to slaves in the mines of the Spanish. The swineherd of Trujillo had wielded the sword of God and a new vein of gold and silver in hitherto unimaginable quantities was opened for Spain.

Soon after the victory, the imagination of Francisco's younger half-brother Gonzalo was fired with a new mission. In Quito, in the mountains of Peru, Gonzalo heard rumours of a hidden land of gold to the east, and 'these tales now crystallised around a beautiful and haunting legend—El Dorado: the Golden Man.'[22]

Emboldened by the triumphs he had shared already, the young and vigorous Gonzalo Pizarro felt he was just the man to find El Dorado, and used his own newly acquired wealth and that of his compatriots to draw together a powerful expedition of nearly 300 men on horseback armed with cannons, arquebuses and crossbows, accompanied by a complement of Catholic priests, and some 4000 indigenous guides, porters and labourers, and lead it off into the mysterious and uncharted interior of the South American continent.

'His goal was threefold. First he hoped to find La Canela, the Land of Cinnamon, which was believed to lie beyond the Andes … Second, he wanted to assess this territory for colonisation. And third, he hoped to find El Dorado, the Land of Gold.'[23]

Despite the elaborate preparations, the expedition hit major problems from the outset, forced to hack its way through endless swathes of impenetrable forest in rainfall that never seemed to cease. When local tribespeople refused to provide information about the Land of Cinnamon, Gonzalo Pizarro 'tortured them—sometimes burning them alive on wooden frames, or casting them to be eaten alive by dogs—including some women …'[24] When they did discover the so-called Land of Cinnamon, the trees were spindly and disappointingly few. Yet he and his men pressed on in search of the ultimate glittering prize, El Dorado.

Conditions only ever worsened for the expeditioners, with baggage and food lost, most of the porters dying from malnutrition and other illnesses, and Pizarro privately lamenting he had undertaken the expedition in the first place. With food becoming more scarce with each passing week—no-one, it seemed, knew how to find enough food in the unfamiliar forest—the members of the party began slaughtering and eating their horses.

After months of hacking through jungle they reached the Coca River where Pizarro had a boat built and, in November 1541, eight months after leaving Quito, set sail downriver in it. But after celebrating Christmas Day with a mass presided over by a surviving priest, the remaining members of the expedition realised they were without any more food, and marooned in seemingly limitless jungle.

The party split up, with Pizarro's one-eyed subordinate Francisco Orellana taking the boat with 60 men down the Napo River to seek food. He never returned; instead, swept along by the swift current, he found himself on a mighty river.

'Orellana ... heard tantalising stories of the existence of a fierce tribe of female warriors, like the Amazons in Greek myth ... the tale gave the river the name it still has today: Rio Amazonas—the River of the Amazons.'[25]

The river turned out to be the world's longest and, in an historic journey of epic proportions, Orellana and his compatriots travelled thousands of kilometres east across the entire South American continent to the mouth of the Amazon, where they emerged into the Atlantic Ocean on 26 August 1542, eight months after parting from the main expedition.

The rump of Gonzalo Pizarro's once mighty Conquistador party had by this time long been subsisting on lizards and snakes, even grilling its saddles and leather stirrups. Turning back west, he attempted to march his remaining followers out of the desperate straits they were in—all thoughts of any El Dorado long gone—skirmishing with tribes along the way back to Peru.

'In June 1542, sixteen months after they had set out, the army staggered back over the Andes. They were emaciated, half-naked skeletons in animal skins ... There were eighty men left ... a miracle so many had survived "the worst journey in all Indies". They had endured as much, perhaps, as it is possible for human beings to take, and still live ... Keeping up appearances until the bitter end, Gonzalo Pizarro refused the horse [brought out to him] and walked all the way to the gates of Quito.'[26]

When Gonzalo returned, his fortune spent, his companions dead, sick or disappeared, and all dreams of El Dorado vanished like so much smoke, he was devastated to receive the news that soon after his departure his elder brother Francisco had been killed in a feud with an old Conquistador comrade in arms, in his death throes drawing the cross in the dust with his own blood, and calling out the name of Jesus.

That was how Gonzalo Pizarro's quest for El Dorado ended, in defeat, despair and heartbreak, but that is not to say that such a place was never found, as we shall see.

✛ ✛ ✛

The gold of the Americas proved problematic for Spain as a whole, the pillaged loot attracting English and French privateers, who in their turn pillaged it from Spanish galleons on the high seas. What did reach the port of Seville was largely dissipated on wars and luxury goods, and in spite of what appeared an inexhaustible source of tapped wealth, Spain was forced to default on its debts in 1557.[27]

Gold and silver were not trucked across the Atlantic in massive quantities for decades, especially after the easiest, initial pickings had been taken. It would take some time before the military adventurism of the Conquistadors could be placed onto a solid business footing. 'Although Mexico fell to the Spaniards in the 1520s and Peru in the 1530s, it was not until after 1550 that the effective exploitation of the new World's resources can be said to have begun ... The newly found territories had to be subjugated, settled, and at least nominally Christianised before the Spanish and Portuguese could hope to create on the other side of the Atlantic viable societies in the image of their own. Until this was done, America would remain no more than a marchland of Europe, an advancing frontier pushed forward by rival warring gangs.'[28]

In addition to the problems of organising labour and of transportation across vast distances of land and sea, a more thoroughgoing exploitation of South American silver had to await technological advances in mining and refining. Silver shipments to Spain grew massively in the latter decades of the century, valued at more than 80 million ducats in the 1590s[29]—stupendous wealth for the era. Yet, 'by no means all this silver came permanently to rest in European hands, for some of it flowed eastwards to pay for Europe's purchase of Asian luxury products ... ' Little silver 'trickled down' too: 'The mass of Europe's rural population would rarely if ever set eyes on a gold or silver coin ...'[30]

While the failure of the mines of the New World to benefit the peasantry of Europe might not come as a complete surprise now, more surprising at the time was the unprecedented inflation which followed the influx of silver, causing much economic head scratching. 'We see by experience that in France, where money is scarcer than in Spain, bread, wine, cloth and labour are worth much less. And even in Spain, in times when money was scarcer, saleable goods and labour were given for very much less than after the discovery of the Indies, which flooded the country with gold and silver.'[31]

The economic benefits to Spain of its colonies in the Americas might be debated, but there is no doubt that contact with the New World helped transform the old one, not only economically, but culturally. And while Rome might have received little direct benefit from the colonies—Spain did keep its possessions and bounties much to itself—there were undeniable benefits in other ways.

Rome might not have drunk as deeply from the river of gold of the Americas as it might have liked, but it found its own El Dorado in a far more important regard: followers. While the various Protestant factions confronted it in Europe, Rome outflanked them in the Americas, its missionaries who accompanied the Conquistadors rapidly converting new adherents, creating a new constituency which grew from the hundreds of thousands to millions, and in time, billions.

Figures released by the BBC in 2005 showed Christianity as the world's biggest religion. Around 2 billion people—or one third of the world's population—were baptised Christians, ahead of 1.5 billion Muslims, and almost 1 billion Hindus. Just over half the number of Christians, or 1.1 billion, were Roman Catholics— around one person in six on earth.[32]

The BBC figures also showed how the Americas remain crucial to Catholic numbers. Half of the total number of Catholics in the world in 2005—approximately 541 million—were in the Americas. At the same time ALL of Europe counted together totalled 282 million Catholics, just half the number of Catholics in the Americas.[33] The burgeoning populations of Central and South America continue to have very high proportions of Catholics.[34]

The New World of the Conquistadors became the storehouse of souls for the Church of Rome. With both contraception (other than the Rhythm Method) and abortion banned under the pain of Mortal Sin, Catholic numbers in the Americas can only be expected to swell too. This was the true riches of El Dorado: people, followers, in their many millions. The descendants of the slaughtered and exploited indigenous populations, of the African slaves transported later to work the colonial mines and plantations, and of Spanish settlers, together became adherents of the religion whose leaders, the popes, had proved powerless to prevent the bloodbath and excesses of conquest and colonisation. In the New World, the Roman Catholic Church hit the golden jackpot to see it through the long winter of the Enlightenment, the ructions and transformations of the Industrial Revolution and the enormously destructive national wars of the twentieth century, down to the time of the current pope, Benedict XVI, with his more than one billion followers.

✚ ✚ ✚

If one pope opened the curtain on a century of tragedy in the Americas, as did Alexander VI with the Treaty of Tordesillas, another closed it, in many respects even more dramatically, by the burning alive at the stake of Giordano Bruno. That pope was Clement VIII, and his intervention in the inquisition against Bruno ensured the thinker would die before the new century, that of the Enlightenment, was more than a few weeks old.

The burning of Giordano Bruno took place against the threat posed by the steady advancement of scientific and astronomical views which were counter to those traditionally held by the Church. The Polish astronomer Nicholas Copernicus (1473–1543) had held (with Pythagorus long before him) that it is not the Earth at the centre of the solar system (and thus the universe), but the sun. Wisely he saved his most contentious views for publication after his death in his *De revolutionibus orbium*.

The German Lutheran Johann Kepler (1571–1630) followed in his footsteps, propounding views of planetary motion which were soon to inspire Newton towards his universal laws of gravitation, while Kepler's Catholic contemporary, the great Italian pioneer astronomer Galileo Galilei (1564–1642), risked his life for decades endorsing the views of Copernicus. He was hauled before the Inquisition and forced on pain of torture to recant things he held to be the truth. In 1633, at the age of nearly 70, Galileo was tried for heresy, after which he became blind, and he died a few years later.

Giordano Bruno was born Filippo Bruno near Naples in 1548, into the family of a soldier. He was sent to Naples in his teens where he studied philosophy, impressing his teachers. In 1565 he entered the Dominican Order and took the name Giordano, and seven years later was ordained a priest. He had read works by Erasmus, by then proscribed by the Index, and his indiscretions of philosophical enquiry led to accusations of heresy and a trumped up charge of murder.

In 1576 he left the Dominican Order and travelled through northern Italy, Switzerland and France—attracting more official religious opprobrium along the way—before settling in Paris, where his free thinking gained him the protection of the king, Henry III. He published books of philosophy and *The Candlemaker*, a comic satire on corruption and hypocrisy in his native Naples. He went on to England, where he briefly lectured at Oxford on philosophy and Copernican theories of astronomy, before moving down to London where he was invited to the court of the queen, Elizabeth I.

There he continued to affirm that the sun is at the centre of the solar system, his adamant heliocentrism earning him quarrels with some of the leading English scholars of the day. He went further than Copernicus by theorising about an infinite universe and the possibility of other worlds, and spoke out against the notion that humanity and nature were separate entities. He also advocated an atomic basis to matter, which was anathema to prevailing Catholic dogma.

In addition to publishing philosophical writings, Bruno followed the banned Erasmus by vigorously satirising superstition and hypocrisy. His view of the Bible as simply a collection of stories and not literal truth, and the doubt he cast upon such dogma as the virgin birth of Jesus, were treated as outrageous heresies by Rome. The 'universal man' and humanist freethinker who coined the phrase 'libertes philosophica'—the freedom to think and to question—was not to be tolerated.

He returned to Paris in 1585, but soon was embroiled in more controversy, and travelled on through Germany, lecturing and writing philosophical texts and poetry until in 1591, homesick for Italy, he accepted an invitation to return there from a friend, a wealthy Venetian called Giovanni Mocenigo. For a time all went well: he even ventured to Padua to lecture before returning to Venice where he engaged in discussions with Venetian scholars and nobles, who like him believed philosophical debate should be rigorous, open-ended and free. His downfall came when he decided to return to Frankfurt, and as a consequence Mocenigo denounced him to the Inquisition. Arrested, he was soon extradited to Rome, where in January 1593 he was locked in the cells of the Sant'Uffizio or Holy Office, the Roman Inquisition.

Over the next seven years he attempted to reach a compromise with his inquisitors, and through them the Pope, Clement VIII,[35] pointing out that his views on many matters were not in essence inimical to Catholic dogma. But the Pope demanded nothing less than a total retraction of his views. In the end, Bruno said he had nothing to retract.

None of this should suggest that Bruno might not have dealt with his circumstances differently, and possibly to better effect. He was, in the judgement of author Morris West, 'like all of us, a contradictory character: a muddled philosopher, an arrogant scholar, a boaster and a poet, scared, venal, compromising, and yet, in sum, a figure of heroic proportions.'[36] Yet he was also beyond doubt among the greatest thinkers of his age, and is now considered one of the most important figures in the history of Western thought.

That Pope Clement and the Inquisition tarried so long in murdering Bruno indicates they perhaps silently agreed with much he was saying, but intent upon maintaining control at home and abroad, they would not tolerate such freedom of thought and speech. It was the final intervention of Pope Clement that sealed Bruno's fate, consigning him to the flames as a bold and dangerous heretic. The words he spoke when sentenced would resonate long after his death: 'Perhaps you, my judges, pronounce this sentence against me with greater fear than I receive it.' As he was led away to the stake in the Piazza dei Fiori, he refused to recant any of his beliefs, holding his freedom dear to the end, also refusing a proffered crucifix as the fire was lit under his feet.

It is a sad and perverse irony that the Christians whom Nero once so cruelly burnt alive for their beliefs, had now become so accustomed to burning other people for their beliefs. And while it will inevitably be countered that the Middle Ages were very cruel times and that other leaders brutally treated any who opposed them, it must be remembered that in the case of the Roman Catholic Church, the burning was being ordered by the most senior followers of Jesus Christ whose philosophy of love, compassion and forgiveness was a cornerstone of the faith they professed.

How had this happened? How had Christ's Sermon on the Mount become the Spanish Inquisition of the mad monk Torquemada, the burning of tens of thousands of women as 'witches', and a philosopher reduced to ashes? The common human lust for power, for wealth and territory and for 'glory' would appear to be the answer, a human failing of men who considered themselves more than that. To achieve their temporal ends, the philosophy of a Jewish leader in a far-off desert land had been turned into a dogmatic code enforced with the sword and stake. The authority of the Church was paramount, and the might and glory of one man on earth had become more exalted more than any deity in any heaven. That man was the pope.

＋ ＋ ＋

The burning of Giordano Bruno was worse than barbaric: it was utterly futile. Within a few decades, the English mathematician and physicist Isaac Newton (1642–1727) published his breakthrough *Philosophiae Naturalis Principia Mathematica* (1687). By propounding a series of laws of physics, Newton ventured to explain all physical phenomena, including the orbits of the planets around the sun.

The reverberations were felt around the world: Newton had changed the power over knowledge forever. It was not just a case of humanity no longer being at the centre of the universe, but of religious dogma no longer being at the centre of thought, and that place now held by science. The Enlightenment had arrived, and over time the Church would cede its power to bully and to torture, to kill those who disagreed with its dogma. The vain bonfire of Bruno was the beginning of an end, a ghastly last hurrah.

EPILOGUE AND CLOSE

As observed in previous chapters, around four centuries ago the Roman Catholic Church began a long, gradual decline in power against the ascendant scientific reason of the Enlightenment, the nation states and the banks, and changing political and social structures and cultures. From the seventeenth century onwards, the papacy underwent a transformation from a fearsome office backed by the torture chamber and force of arms, into a global spiritual and ethical guide, a transnational agony aunt. The temporal power of the Pope has all but vanished, beyond his confessional ear to prime ministers and presidents who bow their head reverently before him, and then continue on exactly as they please. The Pope might have a wealth of followers but, as Joseph Stalin noted, a singular lack of army divisions nowadays. The Pope may yet rule hearts and minds, but he can no longer exact tribute in men and gold.

What is the role then of the Roman Catholic Church in the twenty-first century, in the digital age, the internet era? What is the role of its popes in a world of cyber chat rooms and pop twitter, of the cult of celebrity and all other manner of trivial pursuits? And, not trivially, of paedophilia notorious in its own ranks, of terrorism, HIV/AIDS, space-based nuclear missile defence systems, and bio-engineering, with the human race presumably set upon remaking itself in the image of a teenage supermodel. Despite its continuing strength of numbers, does Catholicism struggle for relevance in a world which moves with a momentum that gives scant pause even for love and compassion, much less contemplative self-examination?

Certainly the Church would appear to be striving towards relevance, with gestures like World Youth Day, the week-long international festival in which the pope spreads his arms wide to the youth of the world. By appealing to positive impulses towards peace and justice in young people, the Church tries to align itself with their desire for a better world. But priests and nuns have been strumming guitars for a long time now, and attempts to make the Church appear more in tune with Western contemporary life do not make its message of opposition to contraception and abortion, and of the 'proper role' of women (there are still no Catholic women priests, and needless to say no female popes) any more palatable to modern values.

The Catholic Church sees the need at least to try to update and 're-badge' because it remains under pressure on all sides. The old conflicts with Protestants and Ottomans might not be played out exactly as they were four or five centuries ago, but there remain parallels. In the West, Catholicism finds itself pitted against a plethora of aggressively evangelical Christian fundamentalist sects, which have attracted large numbers of followers in recent decades, bizarrely among them some leading political figures in the United States. Some of these sects have attempted to turn back the clock on the Enlightenment through extreme views such as so-called 'Creationism'.

This is a literal interpretation of the biblical account of the creation of the world and humanity, placing both a mere few thousand years ago. While some might see Creationism as merely redneck or quaintly ignorant, it is in fact a furious and sustained assault upon science and the scientific method, discounting not only Darwin's Theory of Evolution, but carbon dating, fossil records, and well over a century of archaeology and physical anthropology.

Not merely content with promoting such absurdities as cave men riding atop saddled dinosaurs, the champions of Creationism agitate to have it taught to children in schools, alongside real science. So far, common sense has generally prevailed, but if by any chance they were ever to gain the upper hand through their Trojan Horse of the up-market-branded 'Intelligent Design', one suspects they would move to scratch the inconvenient truths of science from the syllabus, and institute a return to fundamental Biblical mediaevalism, and the flat earth of the time of the Borgias. Four hundred years after his death, Giordano Bruno's beliefs would be in peril again, as would Galileo's and, this time, Newton's.

Catholicism also faces rivalry from the other major non-Christian religions. Islam is becoming increasingly popular in Africa, where Catholic missionaries are actively recruiting converts, while in South and East Asia Catholicism still encounters stiff competition from Islam, Hinduism, Buddhism and other Eastern religions, inhibiting further expansionism.

In the West, it finds itself pitted too against an increasingly vocal number who oppose religion per se, people who may see all religion as having its basis in repression, the subjection of women, and the forced indoctrination of the young. We are but tiny humans, they argue, rough creatures barely down from the trees, living on the barest speck of cosmic dust. How are we to know the meaning of all that flies away from us infinitely in all directions, and gain that knowledge from the jumbled, edited, concocted and re-fried yarns, however colourful, of desert tribes far away and long, long ago?

What is the value to humanity, they question, of foolish notions about a human female conceiving and giving birth to a child while remaining a virgin? What is important, in their view, is not gods and demons, angels and archangels, goblins and hobgoblins, but us, each other, that we might all get enough to eat and drink, have a place to live, and stop killing each other over resources, over land, and over religion.

On a deeper level, some people question the very concept of any enforceable codification of philosophical opinion, which they say would be far better left as it is, philosophy. (The cynical rejoinder to that notion is that while there is no money in philosophy, there is a great deal of it in religion.)

But what of faith, and revealed truth? Faith alone was enough for, among others, the eminent author Grahame Greene. Why is the faith he held, and wrote of searchingly and at such length, not enough for us all? The answer, the non-religious say, is faith in what? One may have faith in family, husband or wife, partner, close friends, and faith that when one turns the key in its lock the front door will open.

To have faith in anything, though, requires more than a desire or a need for it, is their argument. If it is to be faith in revealed truth, the question is which one of the many competing truths, revealed by whom, and to what desired end? Children acquire a strong belief in Santa Claus: after all, the story is solemnly attested to by trusted elders, and backed up by a tinsel-ribboned trove of cultural evidence. But as any grown-up knows, Santa is not real. And that is a truth we all must come to face, the critics of religion say: there is no Santa Claus, no free lunch, no cheap ticket out of any purgatory we find ourselves in, no credit card without a limit and a payment regime.

There are as many different truths in as many revealed forms as there are corner shops, they say, but no guarantees at all for those who buy. Open the package and you will see that it is empty, and then you will be told that it is really God in there but that to see God you must have faith. As such the proponents of revealed truth are seen as hiding behind an imaginary curtain against reality, not realising, like the Wizard of Oz, that the curtain has been drawn aside, and their own sad truth exposed.

So run the arguments of those who oppose religion per se. But whether one agrees with some or any of them, they implicitly raise yet again what is the meaning and purpose of the papacy in our time? They ask what, as he trundles down the byways of our world in his bullet-proof Popemobile, is the real relevance if any to an increasingly materialistic world of this venerable old fellow in white? Is it that he brings us a message of peace, a vision for a better world? Every leader promises a better world, if one chooses to follow them that is. And few leaders have ever brought a message of war, even when starting one. Platitudes do no good to anyone: what is needed is ideas for and commitment to real change.

What the Pope and other leaders might address themselves to is the root cause of the conflicts that have wracked our world with ever greater intensity over the past century, which is the grossly inequitable distribution of the earth's wealth. And they might actively campaign for a fair redistribution of it, starting with the richest nations and corporations, the Roman Catholic Church and the Vatican itself.

And given that our human population continues to grow at an alarming rate, would it also not show true leadership from the Pope to put the size of the Church's flock second, and the future of the earth and humanity first, by agreeing to the practise of contraception? Legitimising the use of condoms by Catholics would be a significant and desperately needed move against HIV/ AIDS too, particularly in Africa where it afflicts tens of millions, and would give the Church's right to life campaigning at least some consistency. And would it not be another important measure to end the compulsory celibacy of the clergy and permit them to marry, which would afford them a deeper understanding of the real lives lived by others in the community, and which some people would argue would be a positive step against the appalling scourge of paedophilia in the clergy.

With three such simple changes, the papacy might yet find some authentic relevance in our world. But these in the end are not matters for myself or any other mortal, but for Rome, and the Pope.

ACKNOWLEDGEMENTS

I am deeply indebted to my historian/researcher, Cheryl Tornquist, although she will be paid in full (and before the afterlife). My thanks also to my darling Belle, who assisted with so many ideas and thoughts, read drafts—and has made me promise never to utter the word 'pope' in the house again after finishing this book. Thanks also to my good friend Stephen Measday in all his many newspaper clippings, Mark Tremlett, Ainslie Cahill, Martin Ford, my agent Rick Raftos, and Diane Jardine, Lliane Clarke and Fiona Schultz of New Holland Publishers.

NOTES

INTRODUCTION

1. Plazas de Nieto, C., and Falchetti de Saenz, A., *The Discovery of Gold in the New World, El Dorado Columbian Gold*, p13.
2. ibid.
3. ibid.

I. IN THE BEGINNING

1. Nero himself lived only into the following year, 68 CE, taking poison after losing the allegiance of his military. His last words were: 'Qualis artifex pereo'—'what a great artist the world loses in me'.
2. The practice is thought to have evolved from early use in Asia by the Persians, and one account has it introduced into Egypt and North Africa by Alexander the Great. The Romans may have acquired it as a by-product from the wars with the Carthaginians. So barbarous and horrifying was such a death that the Romans normally reserved it for political conspirators, non-Romans and slaves, who went to the cross in their multitudes, the Roman general Crassus lining the Appian Way with 6000 crucified slaves after the defeat of the revolt led by Spartacus in 71 BCE. The word excruciating, for inducing great pain, is derived from crucifixion, and unlike some more recent methods of execution which purportedly seek to minimise the victim's suffering, crucifixion was specifically designed to maximise human agony. Crucifixion is essentially death by exposure,

in which a person with open wounds is left to die tormented by insects in the mouth and eyes, birds ripping at their flesh, dogs snapping up at them, as well as the afflictions of sun, heat and cold. Practices varied somewhat across the ancient world, especially with regard to securing the victim to their cross. Victims were often first weakened by the scourging, which all those sentenced to the Roman cross received as a preliminary. Administered by experts using leather whips encrusted with iron balls and sheep's teeth, the scourging opened wounds across the back, buttocks and legs, with considerable blood loss. While in some countries the victim was tied to a cross for the actual crucifixion, the Romans preferred to use long iron spikes, hammered through the hands or wrists and the feet to the cross. The shaft of the spikes could be as wide as one centimetre. Victims died from a number of factors, often in combination, including shock, exhaustion, dehydration, organ and heart failure. Normally they would die in anything from a few hours to three days, depending on their condition before it began, and how badly they had been scourged. Jesus died in three hours. After expiring they would often have their legs broken or their bodies speared by Roman guards, as was the case with Jesus, to ensure they were dead. Bodies were usually left on the cross to be torn apart by scavenging wild animals and birds, the remaining flesh consumed by insects.

3. Tacitus, *Roman Readings*, pp 399–400.

4. The lawyer and later consul Cicero is still one of the most famous figures of republican Rome. His legal practices were akin to those of a modern solicitor or prosecuting attorney, and his speeches to jurors remain among the finest courtroom addresses on record.

5. Pliny, the younger, *Roman Readings*, pp 362–3.

6. Saint Augustine is best known for his book *The City of God*. His other writings concern doctrines such as Original Sin, predestination and salvation.

7. The doctrine of the Trinity relates to a perceived power-sharing arrangement within a single deity, in which the entity called God came to be represented as a triangle, with God the Father at the top, and God the Son and God the Holy Ghost (later, Spirit) at the bottom corners, creating the doublethink of 'God is three and God is one'.

8. The 'transubstantiation' of bread and wine into the body and blood of Christ which forms the dramatic climax to the mass, an act of powerful magic then followed by members of the congregation consuming God, long portrayed by opponents of the Church as a rite with obvious overtones of cannibalism.

9. A sensitive issue when the father of Jesus was Jehovah, or God the Father, and Mary married to Joseph.

10. His extensive writings including his *Summa Theologica* distinguished him among the Church's greatest, if sometimes controversial theologians, and spawned a branch of theology dubbed 'Thomism'.

11. Robertson, A., and Stevens, D., *The Pelican History of Music*, p 149.

12. The Edict also attempted to recompense for past wrongs, returning confiscated property to Christians.

13. Dunstan, W.E., *Ancient Greece*, pp 371–2.

14. The age 33 possessed a magical aura of a kind for generations of devout early Christians, and was considered by some saints the ideal age for their own death.

2. HEAVENLY FRAUD, THE CORPSE IN THE DOCK, AND POPE JOAN

1.   Of note too though is the 'Petrine Primacy', also completely without foundation, cobbled together to make the Bishop of Rome first among bishops.
2.   Chamberlin, E.R., *Cesare Borgia*, p 24.
3.   The State of Vatican City has an area of 0.44 square kilometres. It includes the various palaces and famous museum, archives and gardens, as well as a post office, radio station and publishing house, helipad, hostel, and the barracks of the Swiss Guard. In the year 2000 its population was estimated at 880. The Vatican has its own currency and stamps, literacy is estimated at 100 per cent, but there is no arable land or natural resources. Its form of government is theocratic. According to the *Incredible Book of Vatican Facts and Papal Curiosities*, the Vatican remains childless. 'Though there are women living in the State of Vatican City, no baby has ever been born within the city limits.' p92   http://reference.aol.com/worldmaps/_a/vatican-city/20050502153309990014.
http://www.vatican.va/news_services/press/documentazione/documents/sp_ss_scv/informazione_generale/sp_ss_scv_info-generale_en.html#Ordinamento
4.   Chamberlin, R., *The Bad Popes*, p 11.
5.   ibid., p 13.
6.   Duffy, E., *Saints and Sinners: A History of the Popes*, p 71.
7.   From the website of Fordham University, the Jesuit university of New York. http://www.fordham.edu/halsall/source/donatconst.html
8.   Walsh, M.J., *The Popes*, p 61.

9. The author, thinker and wit of the Enlightenment died in 1788. His last words, upon seeing a candle burning by his bedside, were the mocking 'The flames already?'.

10. Chamberlin, R., op cit., p 20.

11. Walsh, M.J., op cit., p 73.

12. 'A third of the popes elected between 872 and 1012 died in suspicious circumstances—John VIII (872) bludgeoned to death by his own entourage, Stephen VI (896–897) strangled, Leo V (903) murdered by his successor Sergius III (904–911), John X (914–928) suffocated, Stephen VIII (939–942) horribly mutilated, a fate shared by the Greek antipope John XVI (997–998) who, unfortunately for him, did not die from the removal of his eyes, nose, lips, tongue and hands.' Duffy, E., op cit., p83

13. Her name is believed to be derived from Maria, and she is sometimes also referred to as Mazoria.

14. Liudprand, *Antapodosis*, ch xlviii, quoted in Chamberlin, R., op cit., p 27.

15. Chamberlin, R., op cit., p 33.

16. ibid., p 35.

17. ibid., p 37.

18. Some accounts have Marozia finally executed upon the order of her grandson Pope John XII, whose own death in 964 reputedly came while having sexual intercourse with a married woman. John XII, the son of Alberic (the younger), was named Octavian, and after he took the papal name John is credited as establishing the precedent for new popes to take a papal name. Critics have suggested the name change was initiated to conceal lineages deemed unworthy of the papal office, and bad business on the way there. Before the reign of the Theophylacts was over, the papacy had been

bought and sold, and the Emperor called to Rome, in 1046, to officiate on the claims of three different men calling themselves Pope.

19.   Walsh, M.J., op cit., p 76.

3. THE HAIRSHIRT PONTIFF ON THE ROAD TO AVIGNON

1.   According to the *Catholic Encyclopedia*, 'The names "Guelph" and "Ghibelline" appear to have originated in Germany, in the rivalry between the house of Welf (Dukes of Bavaria) and the house of Hohenstaufen (Dukes of Swabia), whose ancestral castle was Waiblingen in Franconia. Agnes, daughter of Henry IV and sister of Henry V, married Duke Frederick of Swabia. "Welf" and "Waiblingen" were first used as rallying cries at the battle of Weinsberg (1140), where Frederick's son, Emperor Conrad III (1138–1152), defeated Welf, the brother of the rebellious Duke of Bavaria, 'Henry the Proud'. http://www.newadvent.org/cathen/07056c.htm

2.   The required majority was set down by the Council of the Lateran in 1179.

3.   Keen, M., *The Pelican History of Mediaeval Europe*, p 207.

4.   Also variously spelled Morone, Murrone.

5.   The *Catholic Encyclopedia* defines 'anchorite' as: 'In Christian terminology, men who have sought to triumph over the two unavoidable enemies of human salvation, the flesh and the devil, by depriving them of the assistance of their ally, the world. The natural impulse of all earnest souls to withdraw temporarily or forever from the tumult of social life was sanctioned by the examples and teachings of Scripture. St. John Baptist in the desert and Our Lord, withdrawing ever

and anon into solitude, were examples which incited a host of holy men to imitate them.' http://www.newadvent.org/cathen/01462b.htm

6. Chamberlin, R., *The Bad Popes*, p 81.

7. ibid., p 84.

8. ibid.

9. ibid., p 104.

10. Like Carthage, Palestrina is of great antiquity, settlements at the site dating back to around the eighth century BCE. Like Carthage too it was destroyed and rebuilt a number of times. Located around 30 kilometres east of the ancient capital, it became a summer resort for Romans, though it was sacked by the tyrant Sulla. Following its destruction by Boniface in 1297 it was rebuilt, but razed again upon the orders of another pope, Eugene IV, in 1437. Rebuilt yet again, it was again sacked in 1527. The hilltop town has nonetheless retained the attractions the ancient Romans enjoyed, later playing host to far less destructive visitors such as the author Thomas Mann, who sojourned there on a number of occasions in the 1890s.

11. Chidester, D., *Christianity: A Global History*, p 234.

12. Keen, M., op cit., p 214.

13. ibid.

14. ibid., pp 215–16.

15. Southern, R.W., *Western Society and the Church in the Middle Ages*, p 44.

16. This followed the brief intermezzo of 1303–05 of would-be peacemaker Benedict XI.

17. Walsh, M.J., *The Popes*, p 129.

18. ibid., p 137.

19. Numerical estimates of deaths in Europe during the Plague

pandemic vary widely, from 25 to 50 million people, or from 30 to 60 per cent of the population.

20. Avignon's bridge across the Rhone, made famous by the traditional song, was of great strategic importance during the Avignon papacy, controlling the route south from Lyon to the Mediterranean, and access to the Palace of the Popes. The song *Sur Le Pont D'Avignon* originated in the 1400s. *Sur le pont d'Avignon/ L'on y danse, l'on y danse/ Sur le pont d'Avignon/ L'on y danse tous en rond*: On the bridge of Avignon/ We all dance, we all dance/ On the bridge of Avignon/ We all dance round and round. The papacy did, in Avignon, for nearly seven decades.

4. HIT FOR SIXTUS: THE PAPAL PATSY

1. Roeder, R. in Plumb, J.H. (ed), *Renaissance Profiles*, p 63.
2. Chamberlin, R., *The Bad Popes*, p 254.
3. Roeder, R., op cit., p 65.

5. BORGIA, THE PAPAL BULL

1. He went on to father nine children in all, by various women, two of them conceived in the Vatican while he was pope.
2. The letter was written in 1460, when Rodrigo Borgia was 29. Quoted in Chamberlin, R., *The Bad Popes*, p 161.
3. Chamberlin, E.R., *Cesare Borgia*, p 2.
4. Chamberlin, R., *The Bad Popes*, p 172.
5. ibid., p 173.
6. Burckhardt, J., *The Civilization of the Renaissance in Italy*, p 109.

7.   ibid., p 109.

8.   Mattingly, G., *Machiavelli* in Plumb, J.H. (ed), *Renaissance Profiles*, p 23.

9.   Chamberlin, R., op cit., pp 184–5.

10.   Roeder, R., in Plumb, J.H. (ed), *Renaissance Profiles*, p 68.

11.   The practice of such Bonfires was satirised a century later by Cervantes in *Don Quixote*, when the priest and the barber try to work out which books of Don Quixote's 'decadent' library to put to the flames.

12.   Burckhardt, J., op cit., p 110.

13.   Chamberlin, E.R., op cit., p 49.

14.   Burckhardt, J., op cit., p 110.

15.   Bull, G, introduction to Machiavelli's *The Prince*, p 17.

16.   *The Borgias: The Art of Power.* http://www.italica.rai.it/index.php?categoria=art&scheda=borgia

17.   ibid.

18.   Johnson, M., *The Borgias*, pp 186–7.

19.   http://www.italica.rai.it/index.php?categoria=art&scheda=borgia

20.   Burckhardt, J., op cit., p 109.

21.   Mattingly, G., op cit., p 23.

22.   Testimony of Johann Burchard, papal master of ceremonies, in Walsh, M.J., *The Popes*, p 155.

23.   These included Rodrigo's great grandson Saint Francis Borgia (1510–1572) a friend of Ignatius Loyola, and among the first Jesuit missionaries, journeying to the Indies and rising to General of the Jesuit Order; and Francisco Borgia (1581–1658), governor of Peru. But after them the dominant line in the family disappears from history.

6. A NEW CAESAR

1. Hale, J.R., *Renaissance*, p 60. Although there is no formal bar on who can become a pope, even today the membership of the papal club remains historically limited to eight countries: Italy, Spain, Portugal, France, Germany, Poland, Greece, the Netherlands and Britain.

2. *The Incredible Book of Vatican Facts and Papal Curiosities* lists the following facts about the basilica. 'Saint Peter's Basilica covers nearly 430,000 square feet, enough for a half dozen football fields, making it by far the biggest church in Christendom. Saint Peter's has nearly 500 columns, over 430 large statues, 40 separate altars and 10 domes.' p 91.

3. Clark, K., *The Young Michelangelo*, in Plumb, J.H. (ed), *Renaissance Profiles*, p 48.

4. ibid., p 38.

5. ibid., p 50.

6. Hale, op cit., p 126.

7. Clark, K., *Civilisation*, p 99.

8. Despite agreement regarding the importance of Michelangelo's frescoes, their meaning remains a matter of debate. This took a decidedly new tack when in 2005 Britain's Channel 4 screened *The Michelangelo Code*, a film by the British art critic Waldemar Januszczak. The title was an obvious reference to the pop-conspiratorial bestselling novel *The Da Vinci Code*, by American author Dan Brown. Januszczak professed an abiding fascination with the Sistine Ceiling—and sought to connect ideas behind the Michelangelo masterwork with, of all things, the Branch Davidian cult of David Koresh, the now infamous religious cult leader. (Intervention by US federal authorities at the

cult's headquarters in Waco, Texas in April 1993 turned to tragedy when 74 people perished, many of them children who were burned to death.) Britain's Channel 4 promoted the film as: '... the product of the detective work and obsessive scholarship by art critic Waldemar Januszczak which spans the last 30 years. During this time he has been trying to unlock the secrets of Sistine Chapel's complex pictorial codes and sumptuous iconography ... Both Pope Sixtus IV (Francesco della Rovere) who built the Sistine Chapel and his nephew (Giuliano della Rovere) later Julius II who commissioned the Sistine Ceiling from Michelangelo were astonishing even in the lurid annals of the papacy. Their story on the one hand is one of rampant nepotism and monumental excess, is also a story of an unshakeable belief that they were to take a starring role in the fulfilment of scripture foretelling the end of the world. This belief in the prophecy is closely mirrored in Michelangelo's masterwork.' This television publicity screed was elucidated by US cultural commentator Charles T. Downey, who quoted the film-maker Januszczak as writing in the Britain's *Sunday Times*: 'What connects the massacre of the Branch Davidians in Waco in 1993 with the birth of printing and Michelangelo and Jerusalem and the Sistine Chapel and that angry minor prophet who wrote book 38 of the Old Testament, Zachariah? It is not, I admit, the sort of question one asks oneself merrily every day. But it is what I forced myself to keep asking as I poked about for the best part of 20 years in the nether regions of civilisation, round and round the houses, in and out of libraries, through Rome, Jerusalem, Bethlehem and a place in Portugal called Evora, seeking to crack the lost code of the Sistine Chapel ... It was, of course, Zachariah who predicted the coming of a character called the Branch, who would rebuild the temple and prepare us for the end of the world. I'm not going to go into any sort of detail here about the Branch and his identity. It's all in the film I have made about the chapel's secret, but I was particularly delighted to track down the origins of the chapel's funny shape—it has the basic outline of a treasure chest in a pirate movie—which was copied from an obscure Christian cartographer called Cosmas, whose chief claim to distinction is that he refused to accept that the earth was round. Cosmas insisted the earth was rectangular, and shaped, as it turned out, exactly like the Sistine Chapel. Am I saying that the popes who commissioned the ceiling and rigorously controlled its iconography were flat-earthers? You bet I am. And Michelangelo would certainly have painted what he was told to paint.' Not the least here, Januszczak is questioning how much artistic freedom Michelangelo really had on the Sistine Ceiling. Traditional accounts give him a great deal: but to reiterate, Januszczak says he was 'rigourously controlled' by Julius, who in effect told him what to paint. Downey goes on to comment that Januszczak's theory regarding Zachariah was prompted by the placement within the Sistine Chapel of the fresco depicting Zachariah—a placement which might elude almost any outside tourist coming in through the visitors entrance, but certainly not Julius and every other pope who would follow him through the papal entrance. Downey notes 'if you enter the place as the Pope does, the first image you would see is Zachariah, and Januszczak has rethought the chapel's decoration from that vantage point.' Downey goes on to summarise Januszczak's theory as 'Julius II believed he was the Branch, a new messiah, predestined

to do great things like knock down old St. Peter's, build the new one, put on armour, and lead an army into war to take back the papal territories. The Sistine Chapel, he says, is a coded message about what the Pope believed was his Biblically ordained destiny. Apparently, David Koresh of the Branch Davidians had the same delusion.' Such a self-styled leader as Julius may well have seen himself as a new messiah of a kind. Certainly, as a pope he was almost larger than life.
http://www.channel4.com/culture/microsites/M/michelangelo_code/
http://ionarts.blogspot.com/2005/05/michelangelo-code.html

7. THE MEDICI AND THE TIARA: LEONINE PRIDE

1. This relates only to the 'major branch' of the family.
2. A refined man with a taste for art, including Titian and Raphael, the Protestant Charles was free-spending and headstrong, with a deep belief in the Divine Right of Kings. His marriage to the Medici princess, a Roman Catholic, led to rumblings among nobles and subjects alike, and helped set Charles on a collision course with the increasingly powerful Parliament. That dispute became ever more fraught, culminating in the English Civil War (1642–1645), with the royalist Cavaliers pitted against the Roundheads, the New Model Army of Oliver Cromwell, the leader of the Parliamentarians. Defeated at Naseby in 1645, Charles was publicly beheaded on Cromwell's order in London in 1649. Henrietta Maria outlived her executed

husband by twenty years.

3. He died at 46.

4. It was Leo I (pope 440–61) who had persuaded the Vandals not to sack Rome when they occupied it in 455, and who three years earlier had persuaded Atilla the Hun (406–453) not to attack Rome. Atilla's push west had been checked in Gaul (France) in 451, in a battle against a combined Roman and Visigoth army on the Plains of Chalons, a defeat from which he was forced to retreat east to what is now Hungary. But he returned the following year and mounted a new campaign against Rome, and on this occasion the Eternal City was only saved after Leo I met with him personally. A number of historians have come to doubt that Rome was indeed spared by Leo's powers of persuasion, considering the disorganisation of the supply lines of the Huns, and a critical shortage of provisions and equipment, more crucial to the outcome. Pope Leo III (pope 795–816) survived an attempt by dissident elements to blind him and cut out his tongue (and thereby disqualify him from holding the papacy). He escaped and went on to be the pope who crowned Charlemagne as Holy Roman Emperor. Pope Leo XIII (1810–1903, pope from 1878) was considered an intelligent and sagacious pope, a force for modernising the Church into the twentieth century. He wrote on social and economic matters. His most renowned encyclical is *Rerum Novarum* (Of New Things) which while denouncing the coming force of Marxism still recognises problems faced by the working class of the Industrial Revolution.

5. *The New Encyclopaedia Britannica* describes the 'Renaissance Man' as an ideal that developed in Italy which: '... embodied the basic tenets of Renaissance Humanism, which considered

man the centre of the universe, limitless in his capacities for development, and led to the notion that men should try to embrace all knowledge and develop their own capacities as fully as possible. Thus the gifted men of the Renaissance sought to develop skill in all areas of knowledge, in physical development, in social accomplishments, and in the arts. The ideal was most brilliantly exemplified in Alberti—who was an accomplished architect, painter, classicist, poet, scientist, and mathematician, and who also boasted of his skill as a horseman and in physical feats—and in Leonardo da Vinci (1452–1519), whose gifts were manifest in the fields of art, science, music, invention and writing.' Another Renaissance Man was England's King Henry VIII. Although by the end of his life an ogre with the blood of two of his six wives on his hands, as a young man Henry enjoyed theatre, wrote poetry and played the lute. Some sources credit him with penning the traditional song 'Greensleeves'. At the same time he was an expert horseman, and revelled in hunting and jousting, all contributing to an image of a well-rounded man, which he was, extremely, by the end of his life.

6.   Chamberlin, R., *The Bad Popes*, p 218.
7.   ibid., p 218.
8.   Burckhardt, J., *The Civilization of the Renaissance in Italy*, p 137.
9.   Waley, D., *Later Medieval Europe*, pp 228–9.
10.   Chamberlin, R., op cit., p 223.
11.   He is also father of the comedian and author Ben Elton.
12.   Elton, G.R., *Reformation Europe, 1517–1559*, p 34.
13.   Interestingly, da Vinci never gained papal favour.
14.   Hale, J.R., *Renaissance*, p 22.
15.   Chamberlin, R., op cit., p 225.

16. ibid., pp 224–5.

17. Rizzati, M.R., *The Life and Times of Michelangelo*, p 26.

18. Chamberlin, R., op cit., p 234.

19. Although much has been made of the resounding rap of his hammer on the door reverberating throughout all Christendom—something modern scholars tend to doubt may even have happened, or else point out that the church door is where priests customarily nailed their notices anyway—nonetheless the reports of Luther's hammer were soon heard in the Vatican, as they were from England to Spain, Sicily to Sweden.

20. Visions of the tribulations of Purgatory tended to vary. Dante depicted it as a cold mountainside where souls wandered ceaselessly.

21. Spitz, L.W., *The Protestant Reformation*, p 15.

22. Elton, G.R., p 19.

23. ibid., p 19.

24. Kohler, W., *Dokumente zum Ablasstreit von 1517*, quoted in Chamberlin R. op cit., p 241.

25. Elton, G.R., op cit., p 19.

26. Spitz, L.W. op cit., p 50.

27. Elton, G.R., op cit., p 35.

28. ibid., p 36.

29. Seward, D., *Prince of the Renaissance: The Life of Francois I*, p 244.

30. Painted in Florence 1502–03.

31. Crankshaw, E., *The Habsburgs*, p 39.

8. THE MEDICI AND THE TIARA: INCLEMENT TIMES

1. Chamberlin, R., *The Bad Popes*, p 255.

2. Alberi, E., *Le Relazioni degli Ambasciatori Veneti al Senato durante il*

secolo decimosesto, p126, quoted in Chamberlin, R., op cit., p 260.

3. Elton, G.R., *Reformation Europe*, p 80.
4. Seward, D., *Prince of the Renaissance: The Life of Francois I*, p 151. Francois bartered his own sons as hostages in exchange for his release, and they would remain in captivity for four years, until the Treaty of Cambrai in 1529, when their freedom was bought with a massive payment of gold. Francois threw fistfuls more of it into the streets after signing the treaty and securing the release of his sons, much to the delight of the citizens of Cambrai.
5. ibid., p 83.
6. Chamberlin, R., op cit., p 278.
7. Clark. K., *Civilisation*, p 125.

9. PUNCH, COUNTER-PUNCH AND THE PETTICOAT CARDINAL

1. Clark. K., *Civilisation*, p 119.
2. Elton, G.R., *Reformation Europe 1517–1559*, p 160.
3. ibid., pp 186–7.
4. After 1917 Baghdad was traded between European powers like a pawn, before becoming the preserve and castle keep of the dictator Saddam Hussein. Then, 86 years after it had been wrested from the Ottomans, it again changed hands militarily, this time to a mixed force under the command of George W. Bush, president of the United States of America, under whose charge the ancient capital spiralled down towards civil war.
5. Seward, D., *Prince of the Renaissance: The Life of Francois I*, p 151.
6. This special meeting (with its unintentional horrid

degustive connotation) was held in the town of Worms, on the Rhine in Germany.

7.   In the *New Yorker* of 17 December 2007, art critic Peter Schjeldahl remarks 'Cranach and his workshop were soon issuing a stream of movie-star charismatic Luther portraits, conveying the subject's vigour and humour, absent his explosive temper. The painter introduced Luther to the renegade nun Katharina of Bora, whom he married. The men were godfathers to each other's children. Cranach's enchanting double portraits of the Luthers countered Catholic characterisations of the match as demonic. As the Reformation blazed through German realms, Cranach stoked it with satirical woodcuts that pictured, for example, the Pope and his cronies spilling from a witch's womb.' p 104. Schjeldahl goes on to mention that Cranach's descendants included Goethe and Manfred von Richthofen, the Red Baron—as well of course as his artist son, Lucas the Younger.

8.   Elton, G.R., op cit., pp 210–11.

9.   Spitz, L.W., *The Protestant Reformation*, p 77.

10.   Elton, G.R., op cit., p 67.

11.   Elton, G.R., ibid., pp 212–13.

12.   Spitz, L.W., op cit., p 114.

13.   Calvin, J., *Confession of Faith*, quoted in Spitz, L.W., op cit., pp 114–15.

14.   Clark, K. op cit., p 119.

15.   Elliott, J.H., *Europe Divided 1559–1598*, pp 32–3.

16.   Elton, G.R., op cit., p 180.

17.   ibid., p 183.

18.   ibid., p 183.

19.   *The Catholic Encyclopedia*, http://www.newadvent.org/

cathen/07639c.htm

20.   'Everything he read in his books took possession of his imagination: enchantments, fights, battles, challenges, wounds, sweet nothings, love affairs, storms and impossible absurdities. The idea that this whole fabric of famous fabrications was real so established itself in his mind that no history in the world was truer to him.' *Don Quixote*, (trans: John Rutherford) p27

21.   De Armas Wilson, D., Introduction to *Don Quijote*, (trans: Burton Raffel) pxiii

22.   *The Catholic Encyclopedia,* http://www.newadvent.org/ cathen/07639c.htm

23.   ibid.

24.   Elton, G.R., op cit., p 198.

25.   The book details a four-week long program of prayers and meditations on matters such as sin, and the life of Christ, which the student or exercisant is taken through by their teacher. Its methods would later gain a wider application through 'retreats', a shorter programme in which exercisants retreat from their normal life in the world, take a solemn vow of silence, and spend a period of days engaged in meditation and prayer. As such *The Spiritual Exercises* occupies a special place in the writings of the Catholic Church.

26.   Elton, G.R., op cit., p 199.

27.   ibid., pp 200–01.

28.   Chadwick, O., *The Reformation*, p 273.

29.   Elton, G.R., op cit., p 201.

30.   Seward, D., *Prince of the Renaissance: The Life of Francois I*, p 245.

31.   ibid., p 246.

32.   Chadwick, O., op cit., p 169.

10. THE HARDMAN PONTIff

1. Soon after taking office he amazed Romans with the intensity of his passion for onions, which he had delivered to the Vatican 'by the cartload'. They might have been less amazed though when he made a teenage intimate a cardinal. 'Innocenzo, who emphatically did not live up to his name, had been picked up by Julius in the street in Parma. The Pope visibly doted on him, and the charitably disposed told themselves the boy might after all be his bastard son.' Still considered a sodomite in some quarters, he is also said to have been an intimate of his namesake predecessor, Pope Julius II. Duffy, E., *Saints and Sinners: a History of the Popes*, p 168.

2. http://www.ladyjanegrey.org

3. The poem by William Hone:
    Young, beautiful and learned Jane, intent
    On knowledge, fount it peace; her vast acquirement
    Of goodness was her fall; she was content
    With dulcet pleasures, such as calm retirement
    Yields to the wise alone;—her only vice
    Was virtue: in obedience to her sire
    And lord she died, with them a sacrifice
    To their ambition: her own mild desire
    Was rather to be happy than be great;
    For though at their request, she claimed the crown,
    That they through her might rise to rule the state,
    Yet the bright diadem and gorgeous throne
    She viewed as cares, dimming the dignity
    Of her unsullied mind and pur benignity.

4. The story of Lady Jane Grey was filmed as *Lady Jane* (1986, director Trevor Nunn), with Helena Bonham Carter in the

title role.

5.   Duffy, E., op cit., p 168.

6.   Elton, G.R., *Reformation Europe 1517–1559*, pp 207–08.

7.   von Ranke, L., *History of the Popes: Their Church and State.*
     Leopold von Ranke is widely thought of as the greatest
     ever German historian. He was among many other things
     a zealous papal scholar, and a great-uncle of the English
     poet and scholar Robert (von Ranke) Graves. Graves's
     biographer, the eminent English critic Martin Seymour-
     Smith, remarked upon von Ranke in the following terms:
     'Leopold von Ranke has been described as "the G.O.M.
     of German historians". He founded a school of objective
     history, which set out to establish sound sources and to
     state the facts. Graves quotes him as saying 'I am a historian
     before I am a Christian', by which he seems to think that
     von Ranke thought the facts were more important than
     faith. Actually his view was that if you recorded the facts
     then Christian Providence would do the rest.' Seymour-
     Smith, M., *Robert Graves: His Life and Work*, p 5.

8.   Derived from the Latin verb 'inquirere', to make an
     investigation.

9.   www.newadvent.org/cathen/08026a.htm

10. Psychological torture methods employed by various
     governments and agencies during the twentieth century
     took root in popular consciousness through depiction
     in works such as Anthony Burgess's *A Clockwork Orange* and
     George Orwell's *Nineteen Eighty-Four.*

11. Estimates vary widely but range up to 100,000 executed, as
     quoted from David Chidester, although according to some
     accounts that number died in Germany alone.

12. One of the best documented witchcraft cases came from

North America, that of Bridget Bishop (c. 1635–1692). The red-bodiced tavern owner so outraged the religious Puritans of early New England that they had her hanged for witchcraft. The first of the so-called Witches of Salem to die, her alleged crime was to evoke feelings of lust in the men of the town. Men swore she had entered their rooms as a succubus by means of witchcraft and encouraged them to indulge in sinful pleasures of the flesh, while others said she flew over the fields outside the town on a broomstick and kept cats as familiars. Her 'artistic' manner of dress, her 'dubious moral character' and the belief that she placed 'young people in danger of corruption', helped seal her fate, and she went to the gallows. Before the witch-hunting hysteria passed, eighteen other women followed her to Gallows Hill, until witnesses began to recant their testimony as delusions prompted by Satan. The Salem witch hysteria remains a gothic chapter in the history of the early European colonisation of North America.

13.   http://www.newadvent.org/cathen/15674a.htm
14.   ibid.
15.   ibid.
16.   Chidester, D., *Christianity: A Global History*, p 292.
17.   ibid., p 293.
18.   ibid.
19.   http://www.newadvent.org/cathen/15674a.htm
20.   Before the plot failed, Lorenzo de' Medici's brother Giuliano had been murdered in front of hundreds of stunned worshippers, during Easter Sunday mass in the Duomo. Dozens more died that day, victims of Sixtus and his fellow schemers. See the chapter 'Hit for Sixtus: the Papal Pazzi'.

21.   http://www.newadvent.org/cathen/08026a.htm

22.   von Ranke, L., op cit.

23.   Chadwick, O., *The Reformation*, p 271.

24.   Elliott, J.H, *Europe Divided*, pp 33–4.

25.   Chadwick, O., op cit., p 271.

26.   In his *Night Letters* Robert Dessaix's character recounts, with more than a hint of irony at the end, a conversation in Venice with a professor about the sixteenth century ghetto there: 'He was provoked into talking to me for quite a while about the Venetian Ghetto, the old foundry not far from the present railway station. Once the Jews were all back inside at dusk, he said, the drawbridges were raised, the gates locked and the shutters on the outer windows closed. Police patrols circled all night. The streets around the Roman ghetto were gated shut as well, but in Rome Jewishness could quite easily leak out into the city—without canals defilement of the Christian body could not be completely prevented. In Venice at night the ghetto was a sealed off island. Christians were safe from the polluting sensuality of the Jew. And the Jew, it must be said, was safe from the violence of the marauding Christian mobs.' pp 131–132. In his Notes, Dessaix remarks further: 'The plan to segregate Jews in the Ghetto Nuovo was first put forward in 1515, and the Ghetto Vecchio was opened for more Jews in 1541. Most but not all Venetian Jews were forced to live in it.' p 204.

27.   Duffy, E., op cit., p 169.

28.   In his Notes to *Night Letters*, Robert Dessaix remarks: 'In 1566 when Pope Pius V ordered the expulsion of prostitutes from Rome and the Papal States, it is estimated that no less than one third of the population of Rome consisted of prostitutes, courtesans, pimps, panders and their dependants. Needless

to say, the expulsion order eventually had to be rescinded to avert economic and social catastrophe. The Church needed prostitution, both to service the sexual needs of her celibate clergy and to supply sinners to whom redemption could then be marketed.' p 205.

29.   For financial and commercial reasons Pope Pius did permit Jews to remain in Rome itself, albeit confined to the ghetto.

30.   http://www.newadvent.org/cathen/11581a.htm

31.   Duffy, E., op cit., p 169.

32.   ibid.

33.   Elton, G.R., op cit., p 208.

11. OLD POPES AND NEW WORLDS

1.   The name is generally considered to have been derived in 1507 from that of Florentine merchant and early navigator of the New World, Amerigo Vespucci (1451–1512), but the origin continues to be debated. http://www.umc.sunysb.edu/surgery/broome.html

2.   Johnson, M., *The Borgias*, p 217.

3.   Turner, J., *Spices*, p 4.

4.   Conquerors

5.   Elliott, J.H., *Europe Divided: 1559–1598*, p 51.

6.   Chadwick, O., The Reformation, p 328.

7.   Chadwick notes re the clergy in the New World: 'The Spanish clergy in America (and the Portuguese in Brazil and Africa) were not for the most part perturbed by the condition of slavery or serfdom under which lived so many of their flocks.' ibid., p 328

8.   Wood, M., *Conquistadors*, pp 15–16.

9.   Lanyon, A., *Malinche's Conquest*, p 93.

10.   ibid., p 93.

11.   Chadwick, O., op cit., p 323.

12.   Wright, R., Stolen Continents, pp 23–4.

13.   'By 1519, when Hernan Cortes and his army attended an Aztec feast on the island capital of Tenochtitlan (now Mexico City) and witnessed the seed in a beverage, cacao was a profoundly sophisticated food. The Spaniards had seen nothing like it. The "beans", as dried seeds were called, were roasted over a fire; crushed into a paste; flavoured with flowers, chillies, black pepper, and vanilla; diluted with cold water, poured between vessels until a froth formed, and served in a lacquered gourd by a train of solemnly reverent women ...' Bill Burford, 'Extreme Chocolate', *New Yorker* magazine, 29 October 2007.

14.   Chadwick, O., op cit., p 323.

15.   Wood, M., op cit., pp 15–16.

16.   'Chocolate was being drunk in Spain a few decades later, and by the sixteenth century was a favourite drink of the rich across Europe.' Burford, B., op cit.

17.   Wood, M., op cit., p 16.

18.   Thomas, H., *The Conquest of Mexico*, p 70.

19.   ibid., p 70.

20.   Cambridge University art and archaeology academic and author Nigel Spivey says that in one massive rite in 1487, 40,000 people were ritually killed in the space of four days in Aztec sacrifice to the sun-god. According to his account, the lines of those waiting to have their chests slashed open and beating hearts cut out atop the stepped pyramids stretched back miles long. Given such customary events,

it might hardly be seen as surprising that the Aztec rulers had neighbouring foes whom the Spanish could recruit in a divide and rule campaign against them, although it has also been noted that human sacrifice was not confined to the Aztecs in the Americas at the time. While Spivey puts the view that such terror was designed to enforce compliance with the political elite, some anthropologists have hypothesised that the flesh of the sacrificed was consumed to remedy deficiencies in the Aztec diet. Prisoners of war were killed in the ritual—scholars have remarked that the Aztecs employed tactics specifically designed to injure for capture rather than to kill their opponents in battle—as were slaves considered lazy and worthless. Spivey, N., *How Art Made The World*, episode 5, To Death and Back, BBC TV, 2005.

21. Chadwick, O., op cit., p 324.
22. Wood, M., op cit., pp 189.
23. ibid., p 192.
24. ibid., p 196.
25. ibid., p 209.
26. ibid., p 216.
27. Elton, G.R., *Reformation Europe 1517–1559*, p 77.
28. Elliott, J.H., op cit., p 50.
29. ibid., extrapolated from table, p 61.
30. ibid., p 61.
31. Grice-Hutchinson, M., *The School of Salamanca, Readings in Spanish Monetary Theory*, 1544-1605 (Oxford 1952) pp 91–96, quoted in Elliott, J.H., *Europe Divided: 1559–1598*, p 62.
32. Approximately one person in six in the world identified as having no religion.
33. http://news.bbc.co.uk/2/hi/4243727.stm
34. In 2005 in Mexico there were 93.6 million Catholics

out of a total population of 104.7 million (89 per cent of population), while in Brazil, there were 151.2 million Catholics out of a total population of 176.9 million (85 per cent of population). One could expect similar proportions in many other Central and South American countries.

35. The Florentine Ippolito Aldobrandini, 1536–1605, pope from 1592.

36. West, M., Introduction to his play *The Heretic*, viii.
As the end approaches and Bruno is offered a prayer-book on the pyre, West has him state: 'I do not wish to pray. Be there a God/ He has a debt to me and, being just,/ Will pay it. If there is no God,/ No prayer, no incantation will assuage/ The monstrous agony of human kind.', p 151.

BIBLIOGRAPHY

Boardman, J., Griffin, J. and Murray, O. (eds), *The Oxford Illustrated History of Greece and the Hellenistic World*, OUP, 2001

Brooke, C., *Europe in the Central Middle Ages 962–1154*, Longman, London, 1977

Bull, G., Introduction to Machiavelli's *The Prince*, Penguin, Ringwood, 1971

Burckhardt, J., *The Civilization of the Renaissance in Italy*, Mentor, New York City, 1960

Burford, B., 'Extreme Chocolate', *New Yorker* magazine 29 October 2007

Castiglione, B., *The Book of the Courtier*, Anchor Books, New York, 1959

Cervantes, M., *Don Quijote*, trans. Burton Raffel, Norton, New York City, 1996

Cervantes, M., *Don Quixote*, trans. John Rutherford, Penguin Books, London, 2003

Chadwick, O., *The Reformation*, Penguin Books, Middlesex, 1982

Chamberlin, E.R., *Cesare Borgia*, International Profiles, International Textbook Company, London, 1969

Chamberlin, R., *The Bad Popes*, Sutton Publishing, Phoenix Mill, 2003

Chidester, D., *Christianity: A Global History*, Penguin Books, London, 2001

Clark, K., *Civilisation*, Penguin Books, London, 1987

Crankshaw, E., *The Habsburgs*, Corgi Books, London, 1972

Dessaix, R., *Night Letters*, Picador, Sydney, 1997

Duffy, E., *Saints and Sinners: a History of the Popes*, Yale University Press, 1997

Dunstan, W.E., *Ancient Greece*, Harcourt College Publishers, Orlando, 2000

Elliott, J.H., *Europe Divided 1559-1598*, Collins, London, 1968

Elton, G.R., *Reformation Europe 1517-1559*, Collins, London, 1967

Elton, G.R., *England Under the Tudors*, Methuen, London, 1969

Grant, M. (ed.), *Roman Readings*, Penguin Books, London, 1958

Graves, A.R. and Silcock, R.H., *Revolution, Reaction and the Triumph of Conservatism*, Longman Paul, Auckland, 1991

Hale, J.R., *Renaissance*, Time-Life International (Nederland) B.V., 1969

Heer, F., *The Medieval World*, Mentor Books, New York City, 1962

Hopwood, G., *Handbook of Art*, Graham Hopwood, North Balwyn, Victoria, 1981

Irwin, T., *A History of Western Philosophy, 1: Classical Thought*, OUP, 1990

Johnson, M., *The Borgias*, Penguin Books, London, 2001.

Jones, B., *Barry Jones Dictionary of World Biography*, Information Australia, 1996

Keen, M., *The Pelican History of Mediaeval Europe*, Penguin Books, Middlesex, 1969

Kittell, E.E. and Madden, T.F., *Medieval and Renaissance Venice*, University of Illinois Press, Chicago, 1999

Lanyon, A., *Malinche's Conquest*, Allen & Unwin, Sydney, 1999

Lasance, F.X., *The New Roman Missal*, Christian Book Club of America, Palmdale, CA, 1993

Leff, G., *Medieval Thought: St Augustine to Ockham*, Penguin, London, 1965

Lo Bello, Nino, *The Incredible Book of Vatican Facts and Papal Curiosities*, Gramercy Books, New York City, 2002

Plazas de Nieto, C. and Falchetti de Saenz, A., *The Discovery of Gold in the New World, El Dorado Columbian Gold*, Australian Art Exhibitions Corporation, 1978

Plumb, J.H. (ed.), *Renaissance Profiles*, Harper Torchbook, New York City, 1965

Radice, B. (ed.), *The Alexiad of Anna Comnena*, Penguin, London, 1969

Rizzati, M.R., *The Life and Times of Michelangelo*, Hamlyn Publishing Group, Feltham, 1967

Robertson, A. and Stevens, D., *The Pelican History of Music 1: Ancient Forms to Polyphony*, Penguin, London, 1970

Schjeldhal, P., Reformers, *New Yorker* magazine, 17 December 2007.

Seward, D., *Prince of the Renaissance: The Life of Francois I*, Sphere Books, London, 1974

Seymour-Smith, M., *Robert Graves: His Life and Work*, Abacus, London, 1983

Southern, R.W., *Western Society and the Church in the Middle Ages*, Penguin Books, Middlesex, England, 1970

Spitz, L.W., *The Protestant Reformation*, Prentice-Hall, New Jersey, 1966

Spivey, N., *How Art Made The World* television series, BBC, 2005

Thomas, H., *The Conquest of Mexico*, Hutchinson, London, 1993

Turner, J., *Spices*, Harper Perennial, London, 2005

Ullmann, W., *A History of Political Thought: The Middle Ages*, Penguin Books, Middlesex, England, 1975

Ullmann, W., *Principles of Government and Politics in the Middle Ages*, Methuen, London, 1966

Waley, D., *Later Medieval Europe*, Longmans, London, 1968

Walsh, M.J., *The Popes: 50 Celebrated Occupants of the Throne of St Peter*, Quercus Publishing, London, 2007

Ware, T., *The Orthodox Church*, Penguin, London, 1963

Wedgewood, C.V., *The Thirty Years War*, Pimlico, London, 1992

Wood, M., *Conquistadors*, BBC Worldwide, London, 2001

Wright, R., *Stolen Continents: The Indian Story*, Pimlico, London, 1993

INDEX

index

about the author

The author of more than a dozen books, Larry Buttrose was born in Adelaide, South Australia and began writing in his teens. He graduated from the University of Adelaide—where as an anthropology student he studied global religions and philosophies—became a journalist with the ABC, and later a freelance writer. A poet, novelist, travel writer and essayist, he is also a playwright and screenwriter. He has published several nonfiction books with New Holland, the most recent being *Dead Famous: Deaths of the Famous and Famous Deaths* (2007), and is currently doing a PhD at the University of Adelaide.

First published in Australia in 2009 by
New Holland Publishers (Australia) Pty Ltd
Sydney · Auckland · London · Cape Town

www.newholland.com.au

1/66 Gibbes Street Chatswood NSW 2067 Australia
218 Lake Road Northcote Auckland New Zealand
86 Edgware Road London W2 2EA United Kingdom
80 McKenzie Street Cape Town 8001 South Africa

National Library of Australia Cataloguing-in-Publication entry:

    Buttrose, Larry.
    Tales of the popes : from Eden to El Dorado, an infamous history /
    Larry Buttrose.
    9781741106664

    Popes.
    Papacy.

    262.13

Publisher: Fiona Schultz
Publishing manager: Lliane Clarke
Project editor: Diane Jardine
Internal design: Natasha Hayles
Cover design: Tania Gomes
Production manager: Linda Bottari
Printer: KHL Printing Co. Pte., Singapore